Finding My Why

Finding My Why

Forgiveness But No Apology

Tasha Y. Berry

NEW YORK

LONDON • NASHVILLE • MELBOURNE • VANCOUVER

Finding My Why

Forgiveness But No Apology

Published in New York, New York, by Morgan James Publishing. Morgan James is a trademark of Morgan James, LLC. www.MorganJamesPublishing.com

ISBN 9781631952869 paperback
ISBN 9781631952876 eBook
Library of Congress Control Number: 2020943052

Cover and Interior Design by:
Chris Treccani
www.3dogcreative.net

Morgan James is a proud partner of Habitat for Humanity Peninsula and Greater Williamsburg. Partners in building since 2006.

Get involved today! Visit
MorganJamesPublishing.com/giving-back

To my children:

Delane: When I first looked on your face I knew my life had changed for the better. You gave me direction in this life. Your journey humbles/inspires me and I'm so glad to have you in my life. I love you dearly!

Bria: You inspire me every day. To watch you grow from a little girl to a proud, confident, successful, intelligent woman and mother fills me with joy. I count myself truly blessed, to share in your life, to share your sorrows and joys as my own. I love you dearly!

To my grandson Phoenix and unborn grandchildren: My promise to you is the same promise I made to your parents: to make your happiness my priority; I'm committed to your happiness because you are God's gift to me.

To my dad: I forgave you. I prayed you found peace in your last days. (Passed away June 2020 from complications from COVID-19)

To Grandmother Memaw: I love you, Memaw. REST in eternal peace! Your legacy lives on! Four generations. (Passed away June 2020 from complications from COVID-19)

Acknowledgments

To my mother: Thank you for giving me life. I love you dearly.

To my sister Nikki: I will always be your biggest cheerleader. I love you.

To my brother Andre: You were always loved and never forgotten. May your soul rest in Peace! Passed away September 2008 from complications from Epilepsy.

To my nephew Jamar: Your example lights the way for others and I hold you up as a shining model of what faith, passion, hard work, and intelligence can do. You're my nephew but I love you as I love my own children.

To Ms. Rawlings and Ms. Blair: Thank you for your prayers, words of encouragement, unconditional love, and support.

Table of Contents

Chapter One

Earliest Memory

My first memory is from when I was six years old. I was wearing a pretty dress, white ruffled bobby socks, and Mary Jane shoes. My hair was up in three big plaits. I was happy because I felt pretty. I'd gotten all dressed up. It was going to be a perfect day.

We were going to spend the whole day together. I had imagined her taking me out to lunch, and afterward we might go to get ice cream.

But it didn't really matter what we did, because the important thing was that I'd be spending time with my mother. Just the two of us. And because I'd dressed up for the day and was looking and feeling so pretty.

Spending time with my mother alone was always a special occasion.

She buttoned me into my coat and we left for the day. But we didn't go downtown to a restaurant, or any place that served ice cream. Instead, we drove to the hospital.

I don't remember riding in an elevator, or being greeted by a receptionist. I do remember sitting on a bench with my mother in the hospital corridor. I was excited, but also anxious—what were we waiting for? I didn't know why we were there, and I didn't ask. I remember bright lights, too, in the long hallway where my mother and I waited, and doctors and nurses passing by, walking very quickly. It was all new to me, and I took it in with the curiosity of a child. At that time, I had no idea how often I'd be seeing the insides of hospitals, and how much I'd get used to how doctors and nurses operated.

I heard a man call my mother's name. It was the doctor. My mother got up to go with him and I began to follow, but he suggested that I stay outside and wait, so I did. I wasn't worried that I couldn't go with my mother because I had no clue there was anything to be worried *about*. I certainly didn't think the hospital or the doctor had anything to do with me. I don't even remember whether or not I was evaluated before the doctor walked off with my mother.

I don't know how long I remained sitting on that bench in the bright hallway, my feet in their ruffled socks and Mary Janes swinging. At some point my stomach began to growl, and I wished I could have one of the candy bars from the vending machine I'd seen at the end of the hall. Finally, my mother came back.

I could tell that she had been crying. But she acted as if nothing was wrong, smiling warmly at me and making me feel calm.

The next thing that I remember is lying in a hospital bed talking to a nurse who had asked me to choose a flavor of anesthesia. Strawberry and bubble gum were the choices. I always chose bubble gum. To this day I can still taste the too-sweet flavor of that bubble gum anesthesia. It never fails to bring back thoughts of those terrible trips to the hospital.

The first operation didn't happen that day. It might have been days later, weeks, even months afterward. The months blur together in my mind. I would not realize until much later what the doctor had told my mother on that day that had made her cry. I did not know that they had been talking about me, or that he'd told her I had been born with a gigantic congenital nevomelanocytic nevus (CNN), better known as the congenital hairy nevus.

A CNN is a pigmented surface lesion that is present at birth. In my case, it stretched from the top of my shoulders all the way down to my rear end. A CNN is not just a birthmark or a blemish. It possesses a significant potential to become malignant, so the treatment is to remove it, grafting skin onto the surface to replace the skin that has been scraped off.

Though I had no way of knowing it, my life changed on that day. The path that my life would take, for better and for worse, was set.

Most people look back on their lives and pick out the happy memories. The celebrations, the family reunions, the moments when they felt close to other people, or felt happy, safe, and comfortable.

But when I think of my childhood, I see my life as a series of sad times. Painful times. When I tell people this, they think I'm being pessimistic. But I'm not a pessimistic person. I'm just realistic and honest. The painful experiences are the only ones I can remember. And the truth is that I wouldn't change anything about my childhood, from being taunted as a child to having moles scraped off my back in a series of operations from the time I was eight until I turned twenty-one.

Those experiences make me who I am. They make me love the way I love, and they make me passionate about what I'm passionate about. I would not be the person I am today, as a mother, a friend, a mentor and community leader, and a businesswoman, succeeding in a field dominated by white men, if I had not had to overcome these challenges as a child.

When I see that day in my mind's eye—the bright lights of the hospital hallway and the rustle of my dress as I swung my legs from the bench, there are four feelings, four words, that come to mind.

Pain. Ugly. Not fitting in. Lonely.
These are the impressions that color my first memory as a child.

Pain

My experience with CNN involved lots of physical pain. The resection procedures, of which I had over a dozen between the ages of eight and twenty-one, involved a surgeon scraping moles from my back. That was the first part of the operation. Then, to replace the skin that had been scraped away, the surgeon would remove skin from my legs and graft it onto my back. It was one of the hardest and most painful things I've ever had to endure.

But when I think back to that day, that first operation, the pain that most resonates is the pain of heartache. The pain of disappointment.

I'd dressed up for this day, because I was so certain it would be special. I'd slept badly the night before, the same way most children sleep badly the night before Christmas, in anticipation of what was to come. I thought we would finally have a big day out together, just my mother and me. Instead we'd gone to a hospital. Instead of being happy, my mother had cried.

She was given the burden of my diagnosis that day. But I knew nothing but the heavy dejection of realizing we were not going to spend the day hanging out together.

Ugly

I was always sensitive about the mole that covered my back. It covered my entire back, and it was hairy and dark. It was impossible for anyone not to notice it, and other children rarely resisted the impulse to point and make comments. Even being asked something as innocent as what was on my back stung me. I learned early on that I was different, and it didn't take me long to get the message that my moles made me ugly. I sometimes felt like a walking leopard. There was no mistaking them for anything else, anything that was healthy and natural.

I hated taking baths, especially when other members of my family were around. Even taking baths with my brother and sister, both of whom I loved, was unpleasant because of the ugly, self-conscious feelings that bubbled up inside me whenever the moles were exposed. Even when no one said anything, I could feel them looking at the moles, and it seemed I could almost feel how disgusted they were.

Dressing up was one of the few ways I had to feel pretty. When I wore pretty clothes, the moles were hidden. A stranger walking down the street would never guess there was anything different about me. I was just like anyone else.

If, on that day of our big trip, my mother had taken me to see an eye doctor or a dentist, I wouldn't have been as upset as I was that day. But when she took me to the doctor's office and talked to the doctor about my moles, it was just as if I'd been stripped naked and examined by a team of specialists. All the attention was on me—and not my pretty smile, my pigtails, my pretty dress or ruffled socks, either. It was as if everyone were somehow staring at my moles through my clothes.

Here was my secret, the part of myself I had learned—even as a little girl—to lock away and cover up, and this stranger was talking about it. I felt so ugly. As if all of me, my thoughts and feelings and personality, didn't matter. All that mattered was the ugliest, most shameful part of me.

Not fitting in

It was many years before I understood that my sister and brother, both younger than me, had different fathers. And it wouldn't be until I was eighteen years old that I would meet my father.

But from a very young age, I understood very clearly that I was different somehow from my brother and sister, and not in a good way. I can recall my siblings' father visiting, picking up my sister and not me. At that time I did not yet realize that he was not my biological father, and so I didn't understand what it was about me that made him not want to take me home with them.

Naturally, I looked around for reasons why. And it wasn't hard to find something that made me different from my siblings, different from everyone. Children always settle on the most logical solution, even if it may not be correct. I couldn't help wondering if my siblings' father didn't want me because of the moles that covered my back.

Not fitting in kept me from forming close relationships with my siblings. I'm very grateful that I eventually did become closer with my siblings—it would have been natural for us never to really connect.

But it was also very clear that I was a burden to a single mother trying to raise children on her own. Although my healthcare was mostly paid for because my mother worked for the federal government, it seemed there were always problems that cropped up, small expenses that accumulated. My mother's car often broke down and had to be repaired by a mechanic. Little things like gauze and bandages, or the ointment doctors told me to rub on the raw skin on the back of my legs, were not covered by my mother's insurance. For a child who was especially sensitive to feelings of not fitting in, it was not a difficult leap to pick up on the feeling of being a burden to my family.

Lonely

Feeling trapped in my box was a lonely place to be. Staying behind while my mother called for my brother and sister, watching as they got in the car and drove off with their father, was a terribly lonely feeling.

Loneliness would become a frequent sensation during my treatment for CNN. Although the nurses and doctors were very nice to me—I got to know most of them by name, and have kept in touch with some of them even to this day, years later—the operations were painful, and required hospital stays to recuperate.

Sometimes these stays lasted as long as two months. That's an eternity to be alone when you are a child. I can count on one hand the number of visitors I received during those times. All around me I saw children whose parents, grandparents, aunts and uncles surrounded them, arriving each day with balloons and flowers.

Because my mother worked and was raising two children—one of them, my brother, afflicted with epilepsy—it was very rare that she was able to make it to the hospital to visit me. Looking back, I can see that my mother did her best with what she had, that she did right by me by getting me the appropriate medical treatment. But to a child, lying alone in a hospital room, the feeling of being forgotten, that no one cares enough to visit you, is very powerful, and for me it has left a lasting impression of deep loneliness.

Sad memories or not, I wouldn't trade any of the experiences, which have molded me and provided me with a lifetime of motivation. Today, when I think of each of those feelings, I'm able to flip each feeling around and identify how I've changed, grown, and gotten strong as a result of each part of my experience.

The main thing I've learned through all my experience is that with every moment and every choice, I have an influence on the way my life unfolds. I've come to see that that's true for everyone. Instead of being a victim of circumstance, a person can find ways to utilize each circumstance for meaningful, positive purposes. That is the discovery I've made as I've gone through my life that has allowed me to take all these negatives and make up my mind to turn them into positives.

Pain. I've experienced the worst pain—physically and emotionally—that I can imagine. My pain is shocking to others. They don't understand how I endured it. Today I know that the only pain that can truly hurt me now is the pain of disappointment because of the high expectations of others. And even that pain I am no longer afraid of, because I've experienced it already.

Ugly. As I gained confidence and became a woman, I entered into relationships with men and discovered that there were people who would love me because of who I was, the self that I projected into the world, and who weren't put off or repulsed by the scars on my back or legs. Those men loved me regardless of my physical scars, and once I started receiving their love, the word *ugly* no longer had any power over me.

Fitting in. When I went out on my own, starting my own business, I gave up worrying about whether I fit in or not. By that time in my life I had proven to myself and others that I was strong, independent, and a natural leader. As a successful business owner and mentor, I set the tone and create opportunities for myself. Today, it's much more common when I take a business meeting for others to fit in with my expectations and requirements. I don't need to fit in—nor do I want to. I'd rather lead.

Lonely. Today I am surrounded by family, by friends, by people in the community. I'm in constant contact with employees, business partners, and prospective clients, and I hear frequently from people seeking my advice. Rarely am I lonely. But my real strength is in not fearing loneliness. As with pain, I have endured it, and I know it will not hurt me. So I am not afraid of being alone, and even seek out solitude, because I know that I can connect with others when I need to, and that there are many, many people who care about me, too many to ever feel lonely again.

It is fitting that my earliest memory should be one with so many negative elements, so many painful associations. In so many ways, that first memory has set the tone for my entire life. It is the start of a life of obstacles and struggles, of pain suffered, but ultimately overcome.

Ships don't sink because they are surrounded by water. Ships sink when they let water inside. One of the most important lessons I've learned in my life is not to let the things that happen around me get inside me and weigh me down.

These obstacles and pains have made me who I am. And I am very proud to look back at those negative feelings and reflect on the great confidence and strength I have been able to draw from that experience, many years ago, as a little girl.

Chapter Two

Childhood

When I think of my childhood, it's hard to see very far beyond that earliest memory, or past my congenital condition. CNN dictated how I dressed, how I behaved, how others saw me, and even how I spent my time. Until I was a parent and could enjoy summer through the eyes of my children, for example, I never really enjoyed the summer—that was when my surgeries were usually scheduled, as it was the time of year when I could lie on my belly in the hospital for several weeks recovering without having to miss school.

Three words come to mind when I think of my childhood: *Pain. Lonely. Ugly.*

Pain

The pain from my surgeries was incredible. The doctors gave me anesthesia during the actual surgeries, but the recovery periods afterward were excruciating. I'd wake from each surgery in intense pain. My back felt like it had been rubbed raw—because it had. The surgeon had scraped the large mole off, digging into my back to remove every trace of the mole in that area. My entire back felt the way you feel when you fall and skin your knee—the flesh was raw and it burned terribly.

My legs were also on fire because the surgeon took strips of skin from my legs and grafted them onto my back. The places where they'd removed the skin looked like strips of red, sizzling bacon.

Recovery was tricky because the doctors and nurses had to treat my back and my legs simultaneously. I couldn't have anything on my back at all while the skin graft took hold except for large strips of gauze dampened with a saline solution that the nurses would come and change every hour. I would lie on my stomach under a contraption I still think of as an igloo, that would let the nurses put a sheet over me without the sheet touching my back.

While that was going on with my upper body, my legs would undergo a very different treatment. They were basically open wounds, and so to help the raw skin there scab over quickly, the doctors would station a heat lamp over my legs to dry the skin. I still remember the sudden, stinging pain when someone would walk by my room, their movement causing a breeze that would hit those open wounds. Something as small as a light breeze could bring tears of pain to my eyes.

The only thing that would soothe the pain on my back was to put a cool saline solution on it, keeping the freshly grafted skin moist and making sure it didn't dry out. The nurses were very attentive and kept my gauze nice and damp, but sometimes things came up elsewhere in the hospital and they were called away, or a shift would change, and it might be an hour or longer before they could come in to change my dressings. When that happened, the gauze would become stuck to my back. To remove it, they'd have to wet the gauze with saline solution as much as they could, then yank it off. The feeling was a little like tearing off a Band-Aid, but in this case the Band-Aid covered my entire back. The pain was excruciating.

Once the surgery was over, I'd spend anywhere from four or five weeks up to two months recovering this way: the top half of my body cool, covered by damp gauze, and the bottom half baking under a heat lamp.

When I was able to go home, it would sometimes take me up to a week to be able to sit down because while the wounds on my legs were drying out and scabbing over, I couldn't bend them. Although I compared the skin grafts to bacon strips, they were several times longer than that, about the length from the tip of my index finger to my elbow. If I wanted to watch television or do anything at all, I had to either stand up or lie on my stomach.

I said earlier that I had somewhere between twelve and fifteen surgeries before I turned twenty-one. To be honest, it may be less or it may be more than that—I simply lost count over the years. As I got older, I became more aware as each summer approached that I would be facing a terribly painful surgery and a long, torturous recovery. That's why I never much looked forward to summer.

In the end, once I was old enough to decide for myself, I stopped going to the doctor. It was abundantly clear by that time that every time I went for a checkup, I'd be told I had to have another surgery. I simply grew tired of the pain and I adopted a philosophy of "What you don't know won't hurt you."

I'd had enough pain. I wanted to go out and live my life.

Lonely

The surgeries I underwent to treat my CNN were long and painful.

But the loneliness that came after the pain could be nearly as unbearable. In some ways, it sharpened the pain that followed my surgeries. When you have no visitors, nothing to entertain you, no one to talk to, it becomes easy to dwell on the pain of recovery.

I'd often be in the hospital up to two months, and in that time I might see three or four people, including family members. All around me, in the other rooms on my floor of the hospital, I'd hear other patients' family and friends visiting them, and look out to see these visitors carrying teddy bears, bunches of brightly colored balloons, and beautiful flowers.

It was hard for my mother to get away and to come visit me because she worked. Beginning when around the time that she reached adolescence, my sister began to get into more and more trouble, and that took up my mother's attention. Often, my other family members simply didn't have a way to get to the Children's Hospital, located near Howard University in Washington, D.C.

It's not as if anyone decided to leave me on my own in the hospital, but the fact was, I spent most of my time there alone. Over the course of many summers and many surgeries, I got to know the doctors by name. I still remember my nurses, Renee and Yvette, who used to take care of me. They tried their best to cut into my loneliness, creating what felt like a mini-celebration when I checked back in for another surgery. They would decorate my room before I checked in, or give me thoughtful presents like stuffed animals or gift baskets full of candy.

But there's only so much a nurse can do. Renee and Yvette had other patients to attend to, and they couldn't sit and talk with me all day. As a result, I spent a lot of my time in the hospital doing nothing, really thinking about nothing.

That continued when I came home from the hospital. Besides needing to recuperate, and to change my bandages every few hours, after every surgery I needed to basically learn how to walk again. Because I'd spent so much time lying on my belly, my muscles had weakened to the point that I had great difficulty keeping my balance and standing up and walking, if I could even manage it at all.

To do that, I went to a physical therapist, but the process required a lot of time. While I was teaching myself to walk again, the summer was passing me by outside. Even at home, where it would have been easy for friends to drop in, I rarely had any visitors for the simple reason that I didn't have any friends.

I watched a lot of television during the time I spent convalescing, and didn't do much else. It was too painful to move much, and for weeks at a time after returning from the hospital I couldn't even bear to sit down. I never picked up a hobby, never read books or drew. If I thought about anything, it seems to me now, I imagined how different things might have been. What if I were pretty? What if I weren't stuck inside? What if I hadn't been born with these moles covering my body?

When surgeries fell during the school year, or when my recovery extended past the end of summer, I would sometimes have a tutor who would come to the house twice a week while my brother and sister were at school. Otherwise, I was home all by myself.

If a family member came home in the evening and asked me what I'd done all day, often I'd have to say, "I don't know." All alone as I was, doing nothing at all, it was easy for the day to simply slip away.

My loneliness manifested in other ways as well, in ways that highlighted the pain of never having known my father.

When I was around age eleven or twelve, the woman who lived next door was moving away and she gave me a bicycle that she was not planning on taking with her. For the longest time, I had the bike in the basement behind a sofa so that my sister and brother wouldn't find it and ride it. Although they were younger, they both knew how to ride a bike. It was just sitting there because I didn't know how to ride a bike. No one had ever taught me.

Because my father was never in the picture, I never had that kind of moment that you see with a father running behind his daughter holding on to the bike, then letting go and cheering her on.

Finally, I decided that not having anyone to teach me wasn't going to stop me from riding a bike. I was going to teach myself how to ride this bike.

I took the bicycle to a street out behind our house that came to a dead end. I got on the bike and slowly taught myself how to push the pedals to move forward. It was a long process, and I kept leaning over with the bike, nearly tipping onto my side, but never quite falling over.

Gradually, I figured out how to make the bike move, and before too long I was biking around that dead-end street in circles. I was proud of what I'd accomplished—with no one to help me, I'd taught myself to ride a bike.

There was a problem, though. In my enthusiasm for getting started, I had not learned how to stop the bike. I didn't know where the brakes were. I kept going in circles, trying to figure out how to brake, until finally I decided I'd have to crash into a gate to stop myself.

To this day, I still have a gash in my knee from where I crashed into that gate: the brake on the handlebars went into my knee as I was thrown over the front of the bike.

But the loneliest part of my childhood is connected deeply to the experience of undergoing so many surgeries. Everything about the experience of undergoing surgery remains vivid to me to this day. To this day, I can't stand the taste of bubble gum because it brings back such powerful memories of the anesthesia given to me before my surgeries.

The anesthesiologist would tell me to count to ten. I'd make a game of it, trying to count higher than I did last time. I can remember getting all the way to nine several times, never all the way to ten. When one of the nurses came in to check on me, counting to ten became a private joke between us: "You only got to five," one of the nurses would say, pretending to tease me.

Because my mother was often away for one reason or another, I had to learn to change my own bandages. My bandages needed to be removed several times a day and replaced, and everything had to be kept sterile. This began almost from the start of the surgeries, when I was nine or ten years old.

Like learning to ride a bike with no one to show me what to do, applying my own bandages took some time to learn how to do. Taking the bandages off was easy enough. Because the surgeries usually covered such a large portion of my back—from my shoulder to the bottom of my rear end—I could reach around and pull the bandages off. When I'd taken the bandage off and removed the gauze, I had to look at the bandages to get a sense of how my healing process was progressing. There'd often be blood and pus on the bandages. The doctors had taught me that blood was good, but pus was bad. If I saw pus, it meant there was an infection—which meant returning to the hospital for an additional surgery. I always hated seeing pus.

Putting on the new bandages was much harder. In addition to keeping everything sterile, I had to wet the gauze with a solution to keep my back from drying out.

I learned to apply the solution to the gauze first, then lie on my stomach and pull the damp gauze until it was in the right position on my back. Then I'd take dry gauze and do the same thing, pulling and shifting both pieces of gauze until they were covering my scars. All of this was made harder by the fact that I couldn't really feel anything against my back because the nerves in the skin had been destroyed—I still can't, to this day. I might feel pressure against my back, but that's as much as I can feel.

Once I had the gauze in place, I'd get up and back up against a wall, pressing the gauze into position to make it stick. This was how I learned to take care of myself in the recovery period following each surgery. Many of my summer memories involve removing bandages and carefully applying new ones.

Eventually I got pretty good at applying my own bandages. But I never quite got past the thought of how strange, even how wrong, it was that there was no one to help me, that I had to figure out something like that all on my own. I never lost sight of how changing my own gauze underlined my terrible loneliness.

Ugly

Summers were never fun for me, growing up. If I wasn't stuck in the hospital, trying hard not to move so that I wouldn't agitate my back or my legs, I was stuck in the house, all alone, with no friends to visit me.

But even when I was well enough to go outside, after I had learned to walk all over again, the summer had some nasty surprises in store for me.

The hardest part about going outside in the summertime was coming in contact with other kids. We tend to view children as sweet and innocent, but the truth is that kids can be terribly cruel. That's especially true when they sense that someone is different from them.

In my case, the differences were plainly visible in the form of the scars on my back and my legs. I simply looked different, and that was enough.

In reality, when I think back on those summers, I can't think of a single time anyone said anything deliberately cruel to me, or even asked what was wrong with my legs. I remember wishing someone *would* ask just so I could tell them that I wasn't a freak, just so I could explain. In a way, silent assumptions and staring were worse than if they'd called me names.

Without knowing anything about the surgeries or my CNN, they were free to imagine the worst. A rumor got back to me one summer that my mother had burned me. Partly that rumor stemmed from the fact that my mother had a burn on her chest that came from a time when she'd played with fire as a child and that covered her skin from the collarbone and down over her chest.

Along with hearing rumors like that, what hurt the most about how the neighborhood kids treated me was being stared at and being shunned. We had a neighborhood cheerleading team, but I was never picked for the team or for anything else because of the way I looked. In the case of the cheerleading team, I've found throughout my life that I've had a much easier time making friends with boys and men than I have with other women. Girls have always been so mean to me, beginning when I was just a little girl.

Being treated like this, of course I began to internalize lots of lessons about myself and how I looked. How could any child, especially a little girl, be stared at and have rumors spread about her and not start to believe that she is ugly?

When we would go to the pool, it was out of the question that I would wear a regular swimsuit, with the back cut out. Instead, I'd wear a one-piece bathing suit and cover it up with a giant white T-shirt that came down to my knees, covering my entire body. Everyone would be diving into the deep end of the pool and playing together, and there I would be in the shallow end, playing by myself.

The pool was the place where I stuck out the most obviously, dressed in my big white T-shirt. If I was outside in my neighborhood during summer, you can bet that I was wearing a big, baggy shirt that covered up all of my back and a pair of shorts that came all the way to my knees. I still remember those shorts: they were from an old pair of jeans that I'd cut off at the knees.

To this day, I can so clearly remember wishing I could wear a tube top, my back exposed, like all the other little girls in the neighborhood. Kids of any time period tend to dress the same, to imitate each other in the way they fix their hair and the clothes they wear. My neighborhood was no different. When I would see other little girls wearing shirts with their arms or backs exposed, I couldn't help feeling left out.

But clothes, and the inability to wear what all the other little girls were wearing, weren't the only thing that set me apart and made me feel ugly. I was always a heavyset child, and that made it hard to dress like all the other little girls.

But even more than that, my nappy hair made it impossible to fit in. When other little girls wore their hair with long ponytails hanging down their backs, or with big ribbons or great big barrettes in their hair, I had no hope of copying their style because I could never manage to grow my hair long. My hair just wasn't naturally silky like theirs, and no amount of ironing, combing, or washing could make it that way.

The feeling of ugliness caused by my nappy hair extended beyond how I felt when I compared myself to the neighborhood girls. It made me stand out even in my own family.

There is Native American blood in my family and because of that my mother, my sister, and a number of other women in my family have jet-black, wavy hair. My mother would pull my sister's hair back into a long, beautiful ponytail. When it came to my hair, however, my mother hated to have to try to do something with it. I can remember a number of Easter mornings when she would dress my sister, my cousin, and me alike. We were all close in age and I was excited to wear the same dress and walk into church all looking pretty together.

But when it came to our hair, once again I was the one who stood out. My mother would prepare my sister's and my cousin's hair in exactly the same way, but when she worked on my hair, she couldn't do anything with it. She'd end up popping a hat on my head. I can still remember how out of place I felt walking into the church with them, the only one wearing a hat, and how clearly different from the rest of my family it made me feel—how ugly.

Over time, my habit of covering myself up extended beyond the summer, beyond Easter services at church. Even when my scars had healed, I took care to wear long skirts or long pants, or permed my hair to cover up my nappy hair. If I was wearing a dress with spaghetti straps, you can bet I had a sweater on over the top of it.

Looking back, I know I learned some of this behavior from being stared at and hearing rumors the other kids were sharing. But I also learned it from my mother. It started with her covering me up. I don't know if it started from her wanting to protect me from other people staring at me and making comments or whether it was because she was embarrassed at how I looked. Regardless, at a certain point I internalized that feeling of wanting, even needing, to always cover myself up. Children are much more observant than we think, and it's no wonder I picked up on these cues and began to see myself as ugly.

One of the most devastating experiences from my childhood underscores just how deeply I harbored these feelings of ugliness, of standing out for all the wrong reasons.

When I was a little girl, my aunt had a boyfriend who'd come around sometimes. The girls in my family used to all sleep in the same bed. There would be three of us in the bed: myself, my sister, and my aunt's daughter. Late at night, when everyone was asleep, the boyfriend would sneak into our room and fondle the girls sleeping in that bed. This was during the time that I was eight years old until I was about twelve. I'd hear him come into the room and I would hear the rustling of the covers as he slipped his hands under the blankets, feeling around for my sister's and my cousin's legs, their thighs, his hands reaching higher and higher, touching them.

He never touched me. Of course, today I'm thankful for that, but as a little girl who already felt so ugly and out of place, I couldn't help feeling jealous. Was I so ugly that this man wouldn't even touch me? The answer seemed to be clear.

(Years later, that boyfriend was caught molesting another girl in the neighborhood and was sent to prison.)

These are the thoughts and emotions I associate with childhood. *Pain. Lonely. Ugly.*

These aren't happy words and phrases to dwell on, certainly. But most of my memories throughout my life aren't happy ones. And as with so many aspects of my life, as I've left childhood behind and become an adult, in control of myself and responsible for my children and for my employees, I've had to consider what kind of hold I am going to let these words, and these childhood experiences, exert over me.

Am I going to continue to feel ugly, alone, and in pain? Or am I going to take these experiences and learn something from them? Am I going to allow the childhood that I had—not the one I wish I'd had or the one I feel I've been deprived of, but my actual childhood—to define my entire life?

The only possible answer to these questions is that no, I'm not going to let my past define me. Yes, I am going to process these experiences and take what I need from them, whatever will help me to achieve my goals in life.

Pain. Today, pain for me is irrelevant. I'm not saying that I'm Wonder Woman, some superhero who doesn't feel pain. But when I feel physical pain now, I simply have no connection with it. It doesn't bother me. There are no instances of physical pain that I can remember, aside from my surgeries.

Even having my two children, I remember nothing about the pain of childbirth. I can recall panicking about the pain of childbirth before I went into labor, not realizing that that pain would be nothing like the pain I felt as a child. In fact, the anticipation of pain before I gave birth was much worse than the pain itself. It was so bad, the doctors looked at my heart rate and were afraid I was going to have a heart attack. They decided to deliver my son by a Caesarean section because it would be safer. I never felt the pain, never felt even a contraction.

What I took away from that experience is that if the pain was not going to be like what I'd felt after all those surgeries, it simply didn't bother me. It's almost as if, going through surgery and recovery over and over again throughout my childhood, I burned out the parts of me that feel pain, that really fear it. I simply have no fear anymore of physical pain.

Heartbreak is the pain that I fear. Much more than hurting my body, what I fear is my heart being broken.

My experience learning to ride a bike is a good example. When I realized I didn't know how to stop the bike, that I was going to have to crash to get off that bike, I didn't fear the pain of it. I knew I was going to crash but I didn't care. I felt happy that I'd taught myself something, and the pain was an afterthought. For as long as I had that bike, I never really knew how to use the brakes. I used to stop the bike by riding alongside a curb and using my feet to slow down. My mother used to ask me how I was wearing my shoes out so fast—it's because those shoes were my brakes. Using my feet as brakes wasn't the most comfortable way of stopping a bike, but it was the only way I knew, and after the experience of the surgeries, I wasn't going to let that pain stop me from going where I wanted to go.

That awareness, and that indifference to pain, has carried me through my career as a business owner and a mother, a wife, a daughter. As a black woman competing in an industry dominated by white men, I've had to develop a single-minded focus, and to put aside fears of pain, disappointment, setbacks. I cannot recall one thing, either material or otherwise, that I decided I wanted, that I was willing to work for, that I didn't eventually get. Not one.

Lonely. A lot of people I know are afraid of being alone. Of eating alone, of spending time alone, but most especially of being seen off by themselves. Especially for a business owner, being by yourself is seen as wasted time, or a sign that you're not making deals, conducting business, building your network.

For me, it's just the opposite. A lot of the strength I have today comes from the simple fact that I'm happy to be by myself. It feels natural for me to just be alone.

Of course, nowadays, if I'm alone, the odds are good that that's by choice. If I'm sitting in a park, under a tree, all by myself, it's because I went there to think and reflect. But the reason I'm so comfortable being alone goes back to all those years when I had no choice but to be alone, when I would have given anything to have friends to sit with, to come over and play with me, or come talk to me while I lay in the hospital.

As I said, I can't change those experiences or make them into anything but what they were. What I can do is take the strength I gained from having gone through them and make something good out of them.

My experience with my surgeries, with recovering in the hospital alone and being home alone all day, has been a blessing in disguise. I'm used to making decisions by myself, for myself, and acting on those decisions without waiting for someone else to come on board or give me their approval. I know that waiting for someone to come rescue me is never going to get me anywhere— I've got to act and make things happen all by myself.

Feeling people watching me has transformed me into someone who no longer cares if my actions make me stand out in a crowd. I'm used to being looked at, to being and feeling different from those around me. The only difference is, today I draw strength from that. I'm no longer afraid of standing alone.

Ugly

As a child, I never felt proud of who I was. For many, many years, long after I was a child, I continued to cover myself up. It didn't matter if my scars became less visible. Often it didn't even matter if a dress or a shirt exposed any of my scars in the first place—I covered up simply by force of habit.

What's changed now is that I've gained confidence in who I am and how I looked. That change comes through clearest when I'm with my children, when I see them reflecting back who I am and how I see them.

My children look at me and see beauty. They are at the top of the list of reasons why I no longer feel ugly today—and why, in fact, I'm proud of my scars. My daughter was about eleven years old when she asked me, "Why are you always covering up?" It was the first time that it occurred to me that my scars didn't bother my children, they didn't bother anybody but me. Their mother's scars were simply there—they meant nothing to them.

That experience, that one simple question, opened me up to questioning a lot about how I had been acting, how I had been treating myself. Why was I so ashamed? If I had their love, what was I covering up for? Who was I covering up for?

Just recently, we all went to Puerto Rico for a weekend vacation. It was a wonderful bonding experience, and for me it was a perfect time to reflect on feeling ugly and feeling beautiful, and to talk about these things with my children. While we were on vacation, I walked around the pool in a tank top and shorts that fell a lot higher than my knees. We sunbathed together and swam in the pool together, and when I got out of the pool I did not cover my shoulders and legs with a towel, as I once would have done. When they were younger, right up to our trip to Puerto Rico, my kids have never felt self-conscious when they're out with me in public. All the time I was there with them, I realized, I felt no shame in my body and in who I was. I was proud.

My children have always made me proud in the way they treat others. They have always been the kind of kids who, if someone at school is different, they'll try to make that person feel less alone. Growing up, my children were always the kind of kids I wish had been there for me when I was lonely and felt ugly. What's truly inspiring is to see that their kindness and compassion can help anyone—even their mother.

My daughter is the kind of person who, if she sees that my back is getting dry, will rub lotion or Vaseline on it because she knows that after years of surgeries, I can barely feel anything on the outside of my back. Of course I wish someone had been there to help me change my gauze and make sure my back didn't get dry, but if I spend too much time wishing things had been different I'm going to miss the fact that I raised a wonderful woman who is kind and loving enough to do that for me now.

As ugly as I felt as a child, I feel just as beautiful now. My scars are all the same, I've just gotten older. Those scars I thought were so ugly before, they're beautiful to me now because they are the source of all my strength and endurance.

Those scars are my childhood. They stole summers away from me, causing me pain, making me feel lonely, giving me such an overpowering feeling of ugliness.

But those scars are my strength now. They are where my strength comes from. Those scars, and the experience they speak of, are a perfect metaphor for my life.

Those scars are my testimony.

Chapter Three

Reflections on My Mother

While I was working on this book, my mother came over for a summer cookout I hosted for friends and family. I welcomed her to my home, and she told me that a photograph of myself I'd posted on Facebook a few days before was beautiful.

I was so surprised that for a moment I couldn't say anything. Part of me couldn't believe it, and part of me was sure she was going to say something more that would undo the compliment.

But no—my mother went on to tell me how beautiful my new haircut was, and asked me where I got it. The next day, she went to that same salon herself. At the cookout, we had a wonderful time.

To many readers, none of this will sound very unusual. When I see my own daughter in the morning, we greet one another by hugging and asking how the other's day was, and if she's wearing a beautiful new outfit, I'll tell her that. As a matter of fact, it would never occur to me *not* to tell any of my children that they're beautiful, or intelligent, or talented, or to embrace them with a kiss and a warm hug.

But that wasn't the way I was raised. That isn't the treatment I was conditioned to expect from my mother. In a way, I have to give my mother credit for my relationship with my own kids: because of the way I was loved as a child, I had to figure out how *I wanted* to be loved. Not just the love I missed out on as a child but the way I wanted to be loved as an adult, and the way I wanted my kids to feel loved by their mother. Sometimes in life we learn just as much from discovering what doesn't work, what we don't like, as we do from perfect behavior and positive role examples.

That's the way it was for me. Attending to my surgical dressings by myself, as my siblings drove away in the car with their father, taught me things I couldn't have imagined at the time. Those experiences gave me a strength I never expected.

I want to make very clear that I love and respect my mother dearly. I'm not writing this chapter, much less this whole book, to settle old scores or to embarrass her. The truth is, I feel closer to my mother at this moment than I have in a long time.

Indeed, I feel I've come to understand my mother better in the last years or so than I have in my entire life. As a mother, I'm able to view things differently, and that includes looking at the love my mother received, and the things that happened in her life that made her the person—the mother—I've known.

When I think of my mother, and our relationship and how it's changed over time, the words that come to mind to describe our relationship in the past are: *Self-centered. Controlling. Entitled. Disappointment. Unapologetic. Burden.* These sound like negatives, but over the course of my life I've found the positive in each of them.

Self-centered

When I look at my mother today, doting over my sister's children, I can honestly say she's a better grandmother than she was a mother. (She's also a better great-grandmother to my sister's grandchildren.)

In the role of grandmother, she's loving, warm, and patient. She volunteers at my great-niece's school. She more or less raised my sister's three children, including my nephew, who's turned into an intelligent and independent young man. He's a husband and business owner, and a homeowner who also purchased a house for his siblings and his grandmother.

If I'm being honest, I have to say that I sometimes get a little envious, watching my mother dote on her grandchildren and great-grandchildren. She never came to my school when I was growing up or volunteered at my children's school. For my senior prom, I had to borrow an old bridesmaid's dress of hers—a purple satin gown with lace, and a faint lipstick stain on the collar. I did my own hair and makeup, and chipped in my own money to help pay for a limousine to the dance. It was not until I was on my way out the door that my mother came home—that's the only reason she saw me before the big event. She and my aunt came running into the house after hanging out and drinking earlier that day.

One of the great comforts of growing into adulthood is that we get second and even third chances to right our wrongs. My mother has done a wonderful job of taking advantage of those second chances to be an important part of the lives of my sister's children and my sister's grandchildren. But to me, that doesn't really matter. I was her first chance to be warm and supportive, to make a young child feel that she is treasured and desired, and she missed it. As a result, I missed my chance to have a loving, caring mother in my life. And in my opinion, she also missed her second chance to be warm and supportive, since she has never treated my own children, who are now ages twenty-five and twenty-seven, anything like she treats my sister's children and grandchildren.

The reason that the word *self-centered* comes to mind is that, as I've gotten older and have understood my mother better, I've come to realize that there was never any evil intent in the way my mother treated me. She never wanted to do me any harm or make me feel any particular kind of way.

The simple fact of the matter is, my mother didn't have anyone but herself. She herself didn't get the kind of love and caring attention that she needed from her mother. Even today, if I'm around my grandmother and the topic of my mother comes up, I'm liable to hear my grandmother badmouth her own daughter. The more of those kinds of comments I hear, the better I understand that for my mother, just as for me, if she didn't focus on herself, and look out for herself—emotionally as well as financially and every other way—no one else would.

In a lot of ways, my mother has never changed. But no one knows better than I do how hard it can be to change your ways, to fight against the urge to be self-centered. I've faced that in my relationships, including my relationship with my husband. It's hard to change. I've done it, but therefore I can't fault others who haven't been able to.

My mother does not have any relationship with my own children like she does my sister's children. They recognize loving, "normal" grandparent behavior because they get plenty of it from their grandmother on their father's side. My mother-in-law calls to catch up, sends cards at Christmas, and invites us over to spend

Thanksgiving weekend with her and the entire family in Ocean City, Maryland. She greets them with hugs, and if she's cooking she'll invite them over to get something to eat. When they get there, she tells them how smart and intelligent they are, how handsome my son is and how beautiful my daughter is. I'm glad they have that kind of presence in their lives, but at the same time I hate that they must recognize my own mother's behavior as the selfishness that it is. But I can't make her change her ways, and I can't make my children love her any differently from how they do. I tell her, "You have to invest yourself and your time in these relationships." It's what I've had to learn in my own life, and it's what I've taught my children. We have to be taught love—healthy love, and how to ask for and receive the love we want.

Controlling

Sometimes as a business owner, I'll recognize my mother in my behavior. As the one who calls the shots, who signs paychecks and makes sure the lights stay on and the job is done right, I want to be in complete and total control.

My mother was and is controlling simply because she wants everything *exactly* the way she wants it. It was that way growing up, and it's that way today.

Again, I'm not trying to run my mother down, and I don't want her to feel bad about herself. As with the other elements of her personality—and mine—there are reasons she is the way she is. When you grow up in an environment where you don't have control over a number of factors, you try to control any element of your life that you can.

This quality has rubbed off on me. It can be useful when it comes to owning a business, but it's also bled into my personal life. A family member remarked to me recently that I spend more time as a business owner and a boss than I do as a wife. And I know I probably spend more time being a boss than I do being a mother. It's something I try to be mindful of. But the urge for control is intoxicating, especially if you've spent a good portion of your life feeling like you lacked it.

Entitled

As I said, over the last several years I've come to understand my mother better. One of the qualities in her that has come to make the most sense is her entitlement. It used to infuriate me the way she would never apologize after we'd gotten into an argument, and would routinely ignore rules or boundaries I tried to set up. I could not accept the idea that simply because she was my mother, she was entitled to do whatever she wanted.

It's been that way as long as I can remember. When I turned fourteen, I was excited to get a job and make some money of my own. But I was always required to turn over part of my check to my mother—sometimes all of it.

Mind you, even at a young age, I understood why she needed the money—growing up in a single-parent household, money was often tight, and a second income, even the little bit that would come from a part-time job, was important. What I resented was that there was never any discussion about it. I was never asked, and my mother never persuaded me that I should do this. It was simply expected.

And in truth, when I got that first job I expected to hand over my earnings because it was just like what happened when I got old enough to watch my brother and sister. I was old enough that now my mother didn't have to worry about being home all the time to watch us, so if she wanted to go out to a bar or to a party, she felt fine leaving my siblings in my care. In time I was expected to do more and more chores, such as cooking and cleaning.

I can certainly understand how it must have felt for her to have a mother who didn't know how to show love, be compassionate, or offer apologies for hurtful things she had done in the past. She also had a father who refused to acknowledge her or take financial responsibility, even as other children he fathered—she had many half sisters and half brothers in town—took his last name, and were even invited into the family. To feel unloved is certainly something I have experience with, and in that regard I can understand how she must feel.

Disappointment

I was conceived from a one-night stand. When I was born, I wasn't a beautiful baby—in fact, I was ugly. I had an ugly black mole covering my back and black spots all over my body. I looked like a black kitten. For a young mother, eighteen years old going on nineteen, how can you help but be disappointed to find that this is your baby?

I can sympathize with my mother, believe me. To be faced with raising a child alone, to look in the baby's face and think that your own child is ugly—how could you not feel that life had let you down, played a trick on you?

I'm sure that disappointment was compounded when I turned six years old and she took me to the doctor, and discovered I'd need extensive treatment for my gigantic congenital nevomelanocytic nevus (CNN).

Growing up, I never heard my mother talk about her hopes for herself when she was a child. A doctor, an astronaut, a lawyer—I never heard anything about her dreams when she was a little girl. I've never known if she had dreams that she never talked about that she had to put away when I was born, or if I was born so soon she wasn't able to form dreams for her own life.

In the years to come, she'd go on to have a son with epilepsy and a second daughter who was a juvenile delinquent and would become a teenage mother. It must have been so disappointing to feel that her only purpose in life was to raise us.

Unapologetic

My entire life, I can't think of a single time that I've heard my mother apologize. Not once.

To me, the sense of entitlement I described earlier goes hand in hand with her unapologetic nature. When you feel you're entitled to receive things, or to act a certain way, why would you feel the need to apologize for anything?

It also goes along with being self-centered. If I were to sit my mother down and tell her stories about a friend of mine who behaved a certain way, and describe that friend doing all the same things my mother has done, I know my mother would never recognize her own behavior. She'd ask me, "Who are you talking about?"

But as with all these other words that come to mind when I think of my mother, I can understand why she is how she is and why she behaves the way she does. She may have felt entitled to certain treatment because she was my grandfather's oldest child, but she had to fight and work for a lot of what she has—including the love and attention of her mother and of the men she was in relationships with. If there's one thing in common between myself and her, it's that we both understand the struggle to be loved, or even simply to be seen.

I've taken a different approach to these things. Part of that approach involves being able to apologize and admit when I've made mistakes.

Burden

Along with feeling like a disappointment in my mother's eyes, I've always felt like a burden. A financial burden to her, especially when I needed treatment for CNN. But in general a burden on her life, her freedom. As I said, no eighteen- or nineteen-year-old girl wants to be taking care of an ugly baby—a bastard child, at that.

More than a financial burden, I was a burden on her heart. I was a burden on her future. I'll never believe that having an unplanned pregnancy and a baby to take care of didn't derail some kind of dream or goal for herself. Even if all she wanted was to keep going out to parties with her friends, going out to clubs, I was a burden on her because she couldn't do that any longer.

The difference between being a disappointment to someone and being a burden is that a burden is continuing, ongoing, a weight the person has to continue carrying. When you are disappointing to someone you have the potential to do better next time, to prove them wrong. But when you're a burden to someone else, it's hard to feel you can ever do right in their eyes or earn their respect.

But treating me like a burden didn't come from nowhere. Even when you're a new mother at nineteen, taking care an ugly baby that's the result of an unplanned pregnancy from a one-night stand, you don't naturally let that little girl feel like she's a weight on your heart. That comes from somewhere else.

My grandmother was also a single mother. In fact, my mother was just the first of seven kids my grandmother had with my grandfather. That's in addition to several stepsiblings my mother has. My grandmother raised all these children on her own. It would be incredible if my mother or any of my aunts and uncles grew up *not* feeling that they were a burden.

These are the words and thoughts that come to mind when I reflect on my relationship with my mother. *Self-centered. Controlling. Entitled. Disappointment. Unapologetic. Burden.*

As I began the chapter saying, I love my mother. I respect who she is and what she's been through. More and more, I feel I can understand the forces and personalities that made her the person I know today—and the woman I knew as a child.

Just as my mother's own experiences with her mother have shaped her, my relationship with my mother has made me who I am today. The difference between us is that I've worked hard to turn all those negative ideas and impressions into positives. By reflecting on what I wished I had received from my mother, and what I could give my children. What kind of love I felt I missed out on, and how I could love others that way.

It took me forty years to cultivate a sense of pride in myself. I could never have done it if I allowed myself to keep feeling like a disappointment and a burden, or let myself be controlled. There came a time when I understood I would never flourish while still playing into others' self-centeredness, or their sense of entitlement, nor sitting around waiting for apologies that were never going to come.

And I would never have developed self-pride if I hadn't come to realize that my worth and my sense of who I am did not depend on who I was with or what I had. No one can ever give you your sense of self-worth, but you can decide if you're going to let someone rob you of it.

You'll never truly feel good until you learn to love yourself unconditionally. Once you start to live from that place, you'll realize that no one can ever take away your most valuable assets—your mind and your self-esteem—without your permission. And you never have to give it.

Self-centered

So many people depend on me. I sign the paychecks for ten employees and five subcontractors, and invoice thousands of dollars each month. I'm the head of our household, I assume the cost of the mortgage and utilities and the household expenses, and take care of all daily maintenance around our home.

It might sound like I'm bragging, or conceited, but those are simply the facts. When you found a company, when you are a single mother, you are at the center of things. So am I self-centered? You bet I am.

I created a life and built a company so I could be at the center of it. The good and the bad of finding business for my company, hiring and firing, paying taxes, and so many other things—I created it.

In my life, I have a lot of commitments, and a lot of people depend on me. I am feeding families. I'm saving souls. The term "self-centered" has a negative connotation—I've used it that way here in this book—but there's a positive side to it, too. Sometimes you have to be self-centered. Sometimes you have to put yourself first, at the center of your own life. If you're going to carry as much on your back as I do, you've got to make sure you're strong enough to do it. And sometimes that means taking a moment to focus on yourself.

Part of knowing your worth is treating yourself well. I tell myself frequently, "I deserve the best that life has to offer." By treating myself well, I reinforce the sense of purpose, discipline, and optimism that guides me in my daily life.

Controlling

When I started my business, I was the only employee. It was just me making phone calls, drumming up business, and contracting out to workers. As a sole proprietor, it was my name that was on the line, and my livelihood. My goal in founding my own business was to take charge of my life and the lives of my children, and make sure no employer ever held our lives in their hands. For every day of those first few years—and, to a lesser extent, still today—every detail has to be taken care of, every contingency and possible mistake or misunderstanding has to be anticipated.

When you're the owner, the founder, and the boss, you can't trust anyone else to worry about these things. You have to out-worry everyone else. You have to take control.

Just like with being self-centered, being controlling is something that has such strongly negative connotations. But sometimes taking control is exactly what you need to do.

Being controlling is something I've learned from my mother. There's no doubt about it. I've tried to harness that desire to be in charge of others, to micromanage them and sweat all the details, for the benefit of my company and my family.

But I've also tried hard to strike a balance between being controlling and being pushy or overbearing. Recently, my daughter, who works for me, sent me an e-mail at work saying that she wanted to take off a Friday. My first instinct was to ask her why. What was she doing? Where was she going?

I had to stop myself. My daughter is twenty-five years old. She is her own person. If she wants to take a day off, she should absolutely be able to do so without her boss wanting to know why.

The fact that her boss is also her mother makes it hard to see those boundaries clearly sometimes, but I strive to keep the parts of my life separate, and to limit my desire for control to business.

Entitled

Now that I'm an adult, I understand that entitlement isn't always a bad thing. Sometimes what we mean when we say that someone is entitled is simply that they have expectations and minimum requirements. As a mother, I've always had standards of behavior that I expected from my children. As a wife, I have expectations of my husband. And as a businesswoman, there are things my employees must do, deadlines they must meet, commitments they must live up to.

Do these things make me entitled? If so, then I'm proud to be entitled. I haven't gotten where I am without keeping promises and meeting, if not exceeding, expectations. I expect nothing less from others in my life.

I'm also secure in my entitlement because I've discovered again and again that the truest fulfillment in life comes not from consuming or receiving, but from creating. You cannot be truly, authentically rich simply by having a certain set of material possessions. The richness that matters is the satisfaction that comes from knowing that you're making a positive difference in life—in others' lives, in particular. Knowing that I've done that makes me all the more secure in my entitlement.

More importantly, where my mother is concerned, I'm secure and confident in letting her know the ways in which I feel entitled to be treated. It took me a long time to be willing to say that. Now that I am, it's important to me that I make sure my children know that they, too, are entitled: entitled to love, to being treated by others the way they wish to be treated.

I don't want them ever to forget that they *are* entitled: to the love that I give them. To the love I didn't have, the love that I wanted.

Disappointment

But by the time you overcome others' disappointment, you're no longer as concerned with what they may think. My mother is proud of me now, and I'm glad that she's proud. She is proud of me because I did all this on my own, because I built something.

The true positive side of disappointment isn't getting approval or praise from the people who were so disappointed in you. It's getting to a place where you trust your own opinion, and trust yourself, and you don't depend on anyone else to know who you are or to value yourself.

Unapologetic

Today, being unapologetic goes hand in hand with all these other positive qualities that used to be negatives in my life. I don't make any apologies for the times that I'm self-centered, or have a sense of entitlement. I'm unapologetic about wanting to control the things around me.

Most of all, I make no apologies for loving the way I love, loving my children the way I love them, or raising them and supporting them in their adulthoods the way I do. That, to me, is the positive side of being unapologetic: feeling confident in who I am, how I do things, and what I've accomplished, and not asking anyone's permission by offering apologies for any of it.

Writing this book, I had to confront questions about myself and my relationship with my mother. I had to get over the instinct to apologize or conceal certain things about our relationship. I had to decide to really become unapologetic for being who I am, and for asking the questions I'm asking about how my mother loved me, why she is the way she is, and why I am the way I am.

At the end of the day, being unapologetic means taking personal responsibility for yourself and your actions. That's the standard I live by.

Of course, that's not to say that I never make mistakes. I'm human and I've made my share of mistakes. In fact, that's been key to how I've learned and grown as a person When I do make mistakes, I try my hardest to own up to them. I try to make up for them, or at the very least let the person or people I've affected know that I've made a mistake. If someone calls me out on something, and they're right, I apologize. To me, being unapologetic makes those times when I do say "I'm sorry" much more powerful—because I only apologize when I really mean it.

What makes it easy to apologize is knowing that my goals are the right ones and my heart is in the right place. Through my creative endeavors, I am trying to transform what I have into the things I desire—for myself, for my family, and for my employees and their families.

In my life, I've found that if you wish to have something of value, you must work to create something of even greater value. That's my goal, and if I fail or go astray in pursuing that goal, I feel comfortable saying "I'm sorry" because I know that my intent was good.

Burden. When you're a burden on someone, that becomes a burden on you as well. You have to live with the feelings of dragging someone else down, of being a drain on them financially, emotionally, and spiritually.

When you can walk away from that, when you can stand up on your own power and support yourself, and free yourself from being a burden, that's powerful. But just as with disappointment, by the time you get to that place you may well find that your perspective has changed.

You might find that you weren't the problem after all. That you weren't as much of a burden as that person made you feel. Or that their feeling that way had much more to do with them than with you. When you get to a place of self-confidence, and are able to support yourself and others, you might ask why that person treated you like that.

For myself, I asked those questions about myself and my mother, and realized that my treatment was not the result of anything I did. Again, it all goes back to how my grandmother treated my mother, the ways my mother learned to treat others, to treat her children, to love and receive love. She taught me to blame myself because she was taught the same thing by her mother. No doubt she felt like a burden on my grandmother.

All those years of feeling like I was the burden, it turned out that the burdens were the things I learned from my mother, the behaviors and attitudes she passed on—probably without even realizing she was doing it. Part of flipping *burden* around from a negative to a positive was in standing up and walking on my own power, carrying myself so no one else had to. But an even bigger part was recognizing the behaviors that made me feel that way, then changing things so that as my children were growing up, they never, ever felt that they were burdens to their mother.

At the end of the day, my greatest fear has always been that I will not be able to provide for myself or my children, that they will end up homeless or having to do without. For more than a decade, I have been able to be the person who is in charge of my livelihood and theirs, without any of us having to depend on someone else. Whether it's a manager who doesn't want to hire them, a company going through downsizing, a government agency furloughing workers during a shutdown, my children and myself have been blessed to be free of the uncertainty and fear that come when your income and daily life are contingent on someone else.

I'm proud that I've accomplished all of that. I wasn't given any of this. I worked for all of it. I didn't wait for life to happen, or for things to go my way. I created life; I created income, and a thriving business that has been one of the foundations of a thriving family—a number of families, in fact.

And I did it all not by turning away from the negatives in my life, but by flipping them. Turning them into positives. There is a positive side to focusing on yourself, to feeling entitled to certain things in life. There is a positive side to always being in control, and to apologizing only when it is authentic and meaningful to the person to whom you're apologizing. There is even a positive side in facing down others' disappointment in you, or their feeling that you are a burden to them.

There is always a way forward, so take it. There is always something useful, valuable, and positive you can do, so do it, and get life going your way.

One of the things I am proudest of in my life is that my mother is still in it. There are a lot of people I know who would have turned their backs, or let themselves grow distant. But I know that as long as we're both alive and she's in my life, there's always a chance to improve things. To take these negatives and turn them into positives.

Chapter Four

Relationships with Men

Until very recently, I have never had a positive view of men, or positive relationships with any men.

First and foremost, that's because there simply weren't many men in my life growing up. For a long time I didn't know who my father was, and to this day I don't have much of a relationship with him—even though, as a little girl, I very much wanted one. In my family, there were many more aunts than uncles: out of six children born to my grandmother, four were girls. Out of the six children all my aunts and uncles had, four were girls.

Will it surprise anyone to learn that I've had difficulty forming strong relationships with men? Trusting them, and really believing that they will do the right thing, has often been difficult for me.

The words and phrases I associate with men are *irresponsible, liar,* and *untrustworthy.*

Irresponsible

In an earlier chapter, I mentioned how I was conceived: my mother met my father in a nightclub. I didn't learn this story until many years later, and for a very long time I didn't know who my father was. All the time I was growing up, he was completely absent, not just in terms of being a presence in the house. I received nothing from him.

Most of the time that I was growing up, in Alexandria, Virginia, my father lived no more than fifteen or twenty miles away, in Maryland. Even if money was tight for him, distance was never an excuse—he could have driven to Alexandria in less than a half hour. I have to assume he simply didn't want to, because he never did.

We did exchange letters, but anytime I put forth the suggestion that we might meet in person, he'd either come up with an excuse or just not respond. He always avoided taking the relationship any further, and in time I came to understand that he simply didn't want a relationship with me. Keep in mind, I wasn't sending him letters begging for money, clothes, etc. In fact, I never asked him for anything. All I wanted was to get to know him—to have the kind of relationship with my father that I saw in girls in my neighborhood and on TV. To be the girl who runs to the door yelling, "Daddy!" when her father comes home and sets down his briefcase.

Each time he failed to write back, each time he offered a flimsy excuse as to why we couldn't meet, I could feel the distance between us growing. For a little girl, that's very hard to accept.

What I understand better now, as an adult, is that that distance came from his inability to take personal responsibility. Just recently I've connected with my older half brother.

We've had some wonderful conversations. One thing I came to appreciate through talking to him is that he hasn't spoken much to my father recently either. My half brother also informed me that his sister, my half sister, has the same relationship to my father as I do. Clearly, the problem isn't unique to me!

In the case of my half sister, I'm able to see even more clearly what the problem is for both of them. When they look at me, they see evidence of the affair he had, and how it led to the breakup of his first marriage. Neither of them can bear to look at me because I'm a reminder of his mistakes. When they look at me they must see pain, disappointment, and heartbreak.

Just recently, too, my oldest brother, my father's son with his first wife, invited me to his wedding. As I write this chapter, I'm deciding whether or not to go. I'm afraid of being a distraction on my brother's big day.

I've often thought that because my father has a degree in psychiatry, because he works with the mind and tries to help his patients understand themselves better, he must have the capacity to understand his own actions, and parse the meaning in his failed relationships. He must be aware of the things he does, must know that these things are wrong. But just as important as your education and what you know with one part of your mind is your character, your ability and willingness to be responsible.

Liar

There is one thing my father has done that still hurts me to this day. As much as I can look at him and evaluate why he acts the way he acts, and in that way try to understand him, I'll never understand how he could serve as a foster parent to numerous children when he could never open his heart or his home to me.

Not only is my father a psychiatrist, someone you might expect to know better, he's been a foster parent for about twenty years. I have the utmost respect for foster parents, those who give a temporary home, love, and support to children who have nowhere else to go. But I can't talk about, or even think about, my father's serving as a foster parent without getting angry and concluding all over again that he is a hypocrite.

What hurts is to picture myself as a little girl, living just miles from where he might be eating dinner with a foster daughter not so different from me. What hurts is knowing he made that decision, to open his home, to give his time, to one of us, but not the other. I'll never accept it and I'll never understand it.

Untrustworthy

I've already described the many ways men have disappointed me by being unreliable and untrustworthy. I've found it's a big risk to put my trust in most of the men in my life.

But my mistrust of men isn't confined to personal relationships. As a black woman who owns a business in a field dominated by white men, I've had a number of professional experiences that haven't done anything to improve my view of men.

As I write this, in fact, I am trying to get a payment of thousands of dollars from the federal government for work that my firm completed. I can be persistent, and my company performed the services it was contracted to do, and I have confidence we will get our money eventually.

But I also feel quite certain that this would not happen to a firm run by a man. Already, in the course of calling different offices, men I've spoken with have suggested that if I drop my claim they will make sure that the next available contract comes to my company, and I'll be paid for that work. I truly can't imagine that person making the same offer to a businessman.

This is just one example of untrustworthiness I've encountered in the business world. My company is named TBS Facility Services Group for a reason. *TBS* includes my initials, but there's a good reason the company isn't named *Tasha Berry Facility Services Group*. TBS stands for *To Be of Service*. Time and time again, we've lined up a contract with a client who's heard great things about our work, is pleased with our price, and in every possible way is looking forward to doing business with us. And in fact, once we've completed the job and done what we said we would do, they're extremely happy with our work.

But before we get to that point, there is almost always a moment when they see a group of mostly black men pull up in moving vans, led by a black woman, and they are taken aback. You can see the second thoughts forming on their faces. What have they gotten themselves into?

In extreme cases, I've lost contracts or had very interested potential clients disappear once they discover that the person they have been e-mailing with, who's provided them a very competitive quote, is a woman. I have learned to deal with it the way I've learned to deal with men in general: by simply accepting that they are not trustworthy, and proceeding from that understanding.

After a lot of careful deliberation, I decided to attend my oldest brother's wedding with my husband. Ultimately I decided that he invited me for a reason, and that took precedence over how my father might feel or what he or his current wife might think about seeing me there.

It was a very emotional day. The anxiety I felt was nearly overwhelming. I didn't know how my father, or especially his new wife, would respond.

But once I got to the venue, I found that the response was positive. Although the greeting from my stepmother felt uncomfortable, it wasn't unwelcoming. My former stepbrother, who I communicate the most with, welcomed me with a big hug and a smile. And my brother, although he was busy tending to his new bride, smiled from a distance—and I was able to sneak in a big hug later on.

My father, on the other hand, was surprised to see me. As far as I could tell, my brother never told him I would be there. And yet his reaction was good: we hugged, and I felt a surge of love that shocked my body. It was a magical feeling.

My husband and I had to leave early due to a prior engagement. Even though I felt relieved by the greetings and hugs I'd received from my family members, once I got into my car, the tears just started flowing. Whether it was due to relief, or happiness, or that magical feeling of love coursing through my body, I wept.

And yet, despite that magical feeling, that shockingly powerful hug, as I write this, several days later, I haven't heard anything more from my father. No phone call, nothing. Even though so much time has passed since I was a little girl, some things haven't changed. On this day, I vowed never to expect anything from him. No expectations, no disappointment, no hurt.

And yet I don't waste time thinking about what might have been or wishing they'd been some other way.

Do I wish I'd had a father growing up? Of course. Would I rather have had someone to run to when I skinned my knee, someone to pick me up, someone to tell me I was beautiful? Absolutely.

But just as I'd rather not have a gigantic congenital nevomelanocytic nevus covering my back, just as I wish my mother had loved me differently, I learned long ago that wishing things had been different does nothing to prepare for right now, for the future. Fixating on how things could have been and should have been doesn't help me provide for my family or show them my love.

With my father in particular, I've been using the fact of his absence and his irresponsibility to drive me for a long time. When I was younger, I wanted to succeed in business because I thought that someday he'd see it and be proud. I wanted to succeed and have him see it, and as I stood up on a pedestal, where my achievements and work ethic had carried me, I wanted to look down and see him looking up at me, noticing me, proud of me—and then I wouldn't acknowledge him.

Today my outlook is different. I've been doing things on my own for a long time now—most of my life. I didn't need him to teach me how to ride a bike and I don't need him to be proud of me now. If I'd had that when I was younger it might have made a big difference, but it's too late now. I'm not going to dilute the pleasure of my successes by worrying one way or the other whether he's proud of me.

Because of the men in my life—whether they've let me or other women in my family down, or whether they've simply been absent—I have a nonchalant attitude toward men.

I don't have male role models, either for business or for my personal life. I love and respect my husband. I treasure my son and nephew, and I'm constantly amazed at the people they have become.

But I don't believe in Superman. I've long since given up hoping for a man in my life to make sure I'm okay. I long ago realized that anything I wanted in this life, I would need to make it happen myself. If I wanted security for my family, whether it be financial, physical, or mental, I would have to go after it myself.

My drive to provide for my loved ones, to succeed, doesn't come from any male role model, but rather from the absence of one. Once I understood I couldn't rely on any man—or, really, anyone at all—I started working to make sure I could rely on myself, and that others would be able to rely on me.

My children, my nieces and nephews, have always been able to depend on me: financially, emotionally—any way I can support them, I have. I've always remained loyal. It's a dedication that stems from my greatest fear: my children not having shelter, or food, or having no one to take care of them.

Because I'm not waiting for Superman, I've had to achieve everything I've achieved through hard work, with the knowledge that I can only depend on myself. At times, that's made relationships with men difficult.

My husband and I struggle now. We've been together nine years now, and married for almost three. Before we decided to get married, we each went to counseling and we also went to counseling together. It was that experience that allowed him to understand that there are reasons for the times that I can be controlling, dominant, even selfish—I had to look out for myself. Counseling also helped me learn to be more compassionate, and to understand that there are times when I need to back down and understand my role as a wife, to accept that I can't be both wife and husband. It can be hard for me to sit back, to do less, when most of my life has been about stepping up and getting things done.

Even now, there are times when my husband may say to me, "I'm not one of your projects. You are not the boss."

Immediately after I was divorced from my first husband, the father of my children, he told me that he wanted to stop using drugs and get clean. I supported him through that process, inside and outside of that facility.

With my ex-husband and his family, I feel blessed to have strong relationships that continue to this day. (And I'm proud that my ex-husband and husband can get along.) I played a key role in helping my current husband transition from incarceration back into society by providing him with a stable, loving place to live and employment with TBS.

At the same time, I feel I've supported both of them, I've challenged both of them to be better men. Not because I want them to live up to some standard that I have in my head, but because I expect it of them. Because this is what I demanded as an example for my children: for my daughter to see a man loving and supporting a woman, and for her to know the feeling of being daddy's little girl, the apple of her father's eye even as a young adult. For my son to see men being supportive and loving to their children, and to see a healthy example of what being a loving and supportive husband and father looks like. I've struggled and worked hard for everything in my life, and my expectations of those around me are high, for men and women alike. These expectations caused me, and others, stress, anxiety, and heartbreak.

My expectations for myself are even higher. I wouldn't expect so much, and I wouldn't know that I am capable of so much, if I hadn't been forced, long ago, to be my own positive role model.

I have learned that in this life you can endure almost illimitable heartbreak, pain, and suffering, as well as disappointment in mankind. Forgive anyone who has caused you pain or harm. Keep in mind that forgiving is not for others. It is for you. Forgiving is not forgetting. It is remembering without anger. It frees up your power and it heals your body, mind, and spirit. Forgiveness opens up a pathway to a new place of peace where you can persist despite what has happened to you.

I forgive you, Daddy, now forgive yourself and create a place of freedom and serenity.

Chapter Five

Adolescence, College, and My First Job

The same words and phrases that come to mind when I think of my childhood—*left behind, lonely, not fitting in*—also mark my adolescence. From junior high school to the day I graduated from high school, those thoughts and feelings stuck with me.

But by the end of my adolescence I had started to do something about that. From my teenage years until the time I got my first "real job" at age nineteen, I was discovering who I was in a way that would set me on the path I continue to walk today.

Around age sixteen, I started working at a CVS nearby, and I had a job pretty much throughout the rest of high school. Working and earning money for myself was rewarding, and it was how I was able to buy my own clothes, get a pager, and give my mother money to help out with the household expenses.

When I turned seventeen, I learned how to drive and got my driver's license. Looking back, I can see that by getting a job and learning to drive, I was moving toward independence. But it wasn't until I went away to college that I took my first big, important steps toward true independence.

I filled out a number of applications and Norfolk State University in Norfolk, Virginia, accepted me on academic restriction. I worked hard all summer to save money and get prepared for college.

I paid for college using a number of grants, plus money I'd saved up from working. When I got to campus, I had a work-study job that helped me pay for some of my living expenses.

In the end, I only stayed in college for one semester. My poor study habits caught up with me and I just couldn't keep up with the requirements. When my sister became pregnant, I decided to leave school to go back home and help her take care of my nephew.

And yet that one semester of college made an immeasurable difference in my life. College was the place where people met me and saw me for who I was. They liked me for who I was, and many of those friends remain friends to this day.

College was the time when I started to embrace Tasha. To be independent, feeding myself and surviving on my own. In many ways, it was a relief because while I was at home I had to act as a big sister and give my mother a part of all my wages. At college I could simply be me.

College was the time when I began to understand how powerful it is to allow yourself to be yourself. When you can enjoy who you truly are and embrace the things you truly love, you can create amazing things. Just as important, when you're authentically yourself, people will respond. It's just a waste of time trying to guess what will earn others' approval or make them like you. I'd learned that lesson through my childhood and adolescence, sitting inside wishing I were popular, wishing I were pretty. College was the time when I began to enjoy being the person I was, being the real Tasha, and saw how the people around me responded.

When I got to college, I was able to let go of Poor Tasha and re-create myself. What began to dawn on me during college is that those bad times, those negative experiences, are part of me but they don't define me.

College was also the time when I recognized that I could be alone without being lonely. I could go to an event by myself and not worry about what anyone thought. I wasn't looking for instructions or waiting for direction.

Looking back on that time now, getting beyond loneliness to a place of comfort with being alone marked the beginnings of my leadership potential. People who can be independent and be by themselves aren't followers. They don't look for instructions, they create instructions and give direction.

Today, I believe that that lesson has helped me immeasurably not just to be comfortable being alone but to be a stronger person. Some people react to loneliness by becoming depressed, others by turning to drugs and alcohol, and still others react by committing suicide because they feel they have to be part of something. Thankfully, I didn't do any of those things, and today when I have time alone it feels like a relief, not a hardship.

I'm okay now with being by myself, and I do a lot of things by myself. Some people may look at that and say, "She's lonely," but I'm simply comfortable being by myself. To this day, I don't have to be around people all the time, and that in turn has given me the strength not to worry too much about what people think, to stand up for what I think is right.

Still, when I returned home from college, I didn't know what to expect. Would I return to all my old patterns and habits? I had no plan, no real prospects. I knew I'd have to go to work, but I didn't have anything lined up yet.

My mother was blunt. "You've got to get a job," she said. She literally made me leave the house every day. She didn't want me sitting around watching television. So when she got up to leave the house and go to work in the morning, I also had to leave the house.

I went all over, knocking on doors and scanning the want ads in the newspaper, filling out job applications and asking if anyone knew of openings. I've never minded working or working hard, and killing eight or nine hours a day is tedious if you don't have anywhere to be.

During this time, I took the civil service test for a job in the federal government. Part of the application process was a typing test. I can still remember practicing every day for that test. The keystrokes and practice exercises became so familiar to me that if you asked me to, I think I could still type them out today. I was motivated to pass the test, and I did.

When I think back on that time, it's almost funny that I was so worried about reverting to the old Tasha. As significant as the changes that occurred during my year away at college were, what I was about to experience was an even bigger shift away from who I'd been before.

Getting my first job with the federal government changed my life. When I look back on that time and the experience of starting out in my first position, the words I associate with it are *relief, excitement, independence,* and *"finally."*

Relief

After all those hours knocking on doors and applying to different jobs, my first job in the federal government came about because of my mother. At the time, she was working in the Department of the Interior, and when a position came open, she helped me complete the application.

The sense of relief I felt when I was hired was incredible. After coming home from college, leaving the house every morning and coming back at night during my job search, I felt adrift. Landing that job felt like I had something to hold on to, a direction to go in.

But starting the job and getting settled in felt even better. My jobs up to that point had been along the lines of a cashier at CVS and telemarketing positions. I had no experience that could prepare me for what a "real job" would be like.

I was relieved all over again to discover that I loved my job. I loved the work I was doing, helping to manage our country's national parks. I loved being in an office from nine to five, Monday through Friday.

Most of all, I really loved the people I worked with. Despite my isolation and the huge amounts of time I'd spent by myself all throughout my childhood, I found that at heart I'm a people person, and always had been. I excelled at the job in large part because I was interested in the people with whom I worked, and I built great relationships with them.

In particular, I built strong bonds with several older women in the department. Those women became my big sisters, my motivators. When I wasn't sure how to proceed with something, I could go to them for advice. In time, I came to seek their advice on matters far beyond workplace issues. One of the ladies even attended the delivery of my firstborn and helped me decorate my first apartment.

In a lot of ways, my work life became more satisfying than my home life, providing me with the support, encouragement, attention, and even love that I wasn't getting elsewhere.

Excitement

Not only was I developing great relationships and enjoying myself on the job, I was being recognized and rewarded for my performance. Whenever I came up for a raise or promotion, I got it. It was incredibly exciting to be encouraged this way, simply to know that the people around me were taking notice of all my hard work.

My supervisors challenged me, pushing me to take on more work and to be more proactive, more thorough. And when I rose to the occasion, proving that I could meet and exceed their expectations, they always rewarded me.

Their challenging me was especially exciting because I had never received that kind of treatment at home, or even from my friends. Never before had someone treated me in a way that sent the message, "I know you're capable of doing more and doing better. Now go out and prove me right." I thrived on the confidence they showed in me, and it drove me to do better and to work harder. Even the simple fact of working in a highly structured environment, with clear guidelines and hours of business, was something new and exciting for me.

I threw myself into the work. The Department of the Interior held a number of environment-focused events, including in-school activities for students, and I volunteered to help out, both in the office and during the activities. When it was time to organize the office Christmas party, I offered to help. It was extra work, and I wasn't paid for it, but I truly enjoyed it.

Independence

For the first year that I worked in that position, I was living at home with my mother, where I was still expected to help take care of my brother and, now that my sister had given birth, to help her with her child.

On top of that, I paid a portion of each paycheck to my mother for rent.

My grandmother was the one who helped me out of that situation. She could see that my mother and I weren't getting along, and that it was likely to only get worse. She told me that I needed to get an apartment, and though I'd given it some thought, I hadn't taken any action to make it happen. It was a big step and I wasn't sure I was ready. I didn't even know where to begin.

With my grandmother's encouragement and guidance, I found an efficiency apartment just around the corner from my office and applied for it. My grandmother cosigned the lease. She even brought me my first Christmas tree. I can still remember her dragging it into the apartment. She helped me finance the whole thing, which my mother wasn't too happy about. Today I'm so grateful for my grandmother's help and her foresight in seeing that my mother and I couldn't live together much longer.

That apartment was another big step on the road to independence that began with my first jobs and earning my driver's license. I was nineteen when I moved out. With as much as I've accomplished in my career and my personal life, it still makes me proud to say that I've never had to move back home for an extended period of time or had to move in with relatives. I've been happy to host relatives and friends who have been between places to stay, or needed somewhere to sleep for a night or a week, but I've never had to depend on anyone else to house myself or my children for more than a month. That first apartment was me getting up on my own two feet, and I've been standing up ever since.

Once I got settled in the new apartment, it felt like I had my own little world, my own life, free of my mother and the obligations of home. I had a steady income coming in—I was making what felt to me, at that age, like great money. It felt like the early days of college again, that sense of freedom that came with being independent.

Even more powerfully, I arrived at work each day feeling that I was being authentically myself. Over the course of my working life, I've found that when you are anxious or worried about the work you are doing, then that work will not be worth very much. But when you can let yourself go and enjoy the experience, that is when you produce excellent and meaningful work.

Other steps, toward even greater independence, followed. I bought a car of my own. I was dating my childhood sweetheart, I had my firstborn child, and soon after the child was born I got married. I was moving further and further away from the lonely little girl who never quite fit in and was always left behind.

While all that was happening, I grew more and more confident in my work. I was promoted to legal assistant, where I excelled, and then to the role of legal secretary.

An opportunity opened up to move up the ladder to the position of paralegal with the Department of Justice, and I took it. By that time, both my children had been born.

Working in the federal government had sparked my social conscience, and I wanted to do good by working in the community. I volunteered extensively, using the skills I'd developed in my job with the Department of the Interior. I helped plan and supervise a large mural of Marion Barry, then the mayor of Washington, D.C., bringing in artists to sketch outlines, and arranging for community members, from children to adults, to paint the mural and fill it in. We used the painting of the mural not only to engage the community but to get neighbors to donate money toward a scholarship fund for local children.

Moving over to the Department of Justice was a tremendous adjustment for me. It felt as if everything changed. I'd been inspired by the work of the Department of the Interior, happy to be part of its mission. At the Department of Justice, I dealt with immigration and deportation issues. Suddenly I held the fate of other human beings in my hands, vested with a power capable of destroying their livelihood and their whole way of life by deportation.

My social conscience, awakened at the Department of the Interior, rebelled at a lot of what I saw as a paralegal at the Department of Justice. What I saw in the court documents that crossed my desk were stories of people who had come into this country and were working hard to provide for their families. My thought was that there were American citizens, even regular people in Washington, D.C., who weren't doing that. But because of their immigration status, a lot of the time, those hardworking people would be sent back to their home countries.

Even more eye-opening was my experience working to prepare the Department for an important case in which tobacco companies were being sued. Here I was, looking at documentation showing that the federal government had known for decades about the risks of smoking, and my job was to help the government prove that it knew nothing. After awakening my social conscience at my previous position, it was all extremely discouraging.

These were among the reasons why I left the federal government and joined AmeriCorps, a government-funded civil society program that encourages public service in the community.

Joining the AmeriCorps was a life-changing event for me. Community service, community development, and doing my part to save our youth made me feel like I was back where I needed to be, doing work that made me feel alive. Once again I felt that I was being useful and helping others.

"Finally"

My sense of "finally" goes hand in hand with the relief I felt once I started that first job, and the sense of independence that grew and grew as I settled into the job and into the life I was making for myself.

Finally, I had a role to play, where my talents were not only put to good use but were appreciated. Finally, other people were taking notice of me and of my abilities.

Finally, others could see the Tasha that I saw when I looked in the mirror. The older women in the Department of the Interior who became my friends didn't look at me and see a back covered with moles, they saw a happy, funky younger girl who liked her job and was a pleasure to be around.

Finally, I was someplace where it wasn't so important to fit in. I didn't look like the other young people in the department. I didn't go out to clubs. I didn't fit in there, either, but I no longer cared because here were people who understood me as I was.

Finally, I was able to come out of my shell. My self-esteem rose through the roof. Men started liking me and talking to me, even men who hadn't so much as looked at me before.

Finally, I was my own person. My livelihood didn't revolve around my mother anymore, or around anyone else. It was on me, and I couldn't have been happier.

Those early years of working at my first real job set me on the path that I'm following to this day.

That job and the feelings of satisfaction and confidence that I drew from it paved the way for me to go out on my own and start my own company just eight years later.

But it goes deeper than that. I can look ahead to the chapters of my story that are still to come and I can draw clear connections between what I'm called to do and the way I live my life and the lessons I learned from my earliest years in employment.

When I look at the way I involved the community in creating that mural in a D.C. neighborhood, helping send youth to college, organizing community development projects, educating youth on community service, I think about the Thanksgiving food basket drive that I now organize each year, where we feed families for Thanksgiving and Christmastime.

When I look at how I felt, holding the lives of immigrants and their families in my hands, I see the desires that kept growing in me to treat the people around me as people, not numbers or files to be processed, and to give back to the community. Not only to be independent, and never have anyone holding my livelihood in their hands, but to take care of others' livelihoods in a positive way, by creating jobs and opportunities for them to build their own lives.

When I look at the way that first job awakened my social conscience, I think of how, today, I literally think I could save the world. That belief manifests itself in my work as a business owner, in my work as founder of a nonprofit organization dedicated to lifting up young men who have been incarcerated, but it all starts with supporting and pushing and cheering on my children. Parenting is the kind of job for which there is no practice. You give it your best shot, and trust that God will make your children resilient enough that they don't suffer too much from your mistakes. I've made mistakes with my children—sometimes I've pushed too hard; other times, I didn't push nearly hard enough.

The rewards of parenthood have been immense. Every day I draw some kind of inspiration, strength, or life lesson from the accomplishments and achievements of my children—but, more importantly, from who they have become in life.

When I look at the confidence that job gave me, I see the pride I take today in leading my employees. I take pride in pushing people to grow, expand, improve, and progress. That goes not only for my employees but the people I surround myself with outside of work. A lot of people have walked out of my life for this reason, but a lot of people have learned to love me even more. The one thing both groups have in common is that they walked away understanding what it meant to push, improve, learn, and discipline yourself if you want to make a real impact in the world.

And when I look at the way that the friendship of those older women in my department first encouraged me and gave me strength, I look at what I try to do now that I'm a grown woman, finding girls who remind me of myself at that age, and providing them with mentorship that will give them the encouragement and confidence I wish I'd had as a child.

I got noticed in the federal government. I became the Tasha I had only begun to see myself as in college. I got a name and an identity all my own.

That was just the start of my transition to who I am today. Through the years since, I've continued to grow, and my sense of purpose—to give back and pay things forward—has grown exponentially since then.

It was those first few years, and that taste of independence, that set me on the path that I continue to walk today.

Chapter Six

Starting a Business

I f leaving home to go to college and getting my first job in the federal government were turning points in my life, what came next was the true culmination of all the change and growth I had been experiencing.

By the time I came to my job at the Department of Immigration, I'd come a long way from the shy, lonely little girl who used to spend the summers indoors. In fact, I was a different person even from the young woman who came back from college with her eyes opened, ready to start out on her own.

I'd been working since I was sixteen years old. In my time working for the federal government, I'd taken charge of projects, taken ownership of my work, and earned the praise and friendship of my peers and my superiors. I'd worked my way up from an administrative assistant to a Paralegal Specialist GS11. Although

I was just twenty-five years old, I was making more than $40,000 a year.

But more important than any of those achievements was what had been occurring within me.

I'd made the important discovery that it mattered to me that I believe in my work, that what I did lined up with my values. When I worked at the Department of the Interior, and knew my work was helping maintain and preserve wildlife, I was happy. When I worked for AmeriCorps, helping to produce a beautiful mural and raising money for a college fund in the process, that made me happy. I might have left those jobs tired at the end of the day, but I left feeling good about what I was doing.

I didn't feel the same about the work I did for the Department of Justice. When I left that job at the end of the day, I didn't feel like I'd done something to help people. I was taking good, hardworking people who wanted to be in this country and deciding whether they should stay in this country or be deported.

On top of that, for a long time I'd been aware—too aware—of how much my position, my entire livelihood and that of my children, depended on other people. How could I not wonder what would happen if I got laid off, if there were budget cuts to my department, looking around and seeing neighbors, friends, family members suffering due to layoffs, cutbacks, or even just the whims of their bosses?

Worker Bee

When I look back on where I was in the summer of 2005, it's no wonder that that was a turning point for me. I was restless. I was ready to do something meaningful, to take a leap into the unknown and make something happen.

But I might not have done it so soon if it weren't for the little "push" I received.

When my boss at the Department of Justice sat me down for my annual performance review, it was a shock. For the first time that I could remember, I got a negative performance review. At all my prior jobs in the federal government, the reports from my bosses had been glowing. Impeccable.

Now my boss was sitting across his desk from me telling me that my work ethic was poor, that I needed to get my head out of the clouds. Apparently my opinion of the work we were doing there, the feelings of disapproval and guilt that I'd been careful to keep to myself, were translating into a slip in work performance.

If my boss had stopped there, things might have been different. I've always taken pride in my work, and I've never minded criticism when it's fair. To be told that my work was lacking was a wake-up call. Maybe I would have buckled down and thrown myself into my work if she had stopped there.

But she didn't stop there. This was a great position, she told me. She said that I was lucky to have such a good government job, and I'd better work hard because I would always be an employee, a "worker bee."

What I heard her saying was that she controlled my livelihood. She controlled whether I would be able to eat, whether I had a roof over my and my children's heads. She had complete control over me.

Immediately after my review, I was transferred to another division within the Department of Justice. It would be one of the last cases I was involved with there.

The case for the Department of Justice was United States v. Philip Morris USA, Inc. This was a famous case where the government held the tobacco company liable for the damaging health effects to millions of Americans who smoked, based on the allegation that Philip Morris had committed fraud to deny that smoking was dangerous.

I was part of the team that went through documents showing that Philip Morris knew that cigarettes caused cancer. We found evidence that the company destroyed documents, paid off doctors and government officials, and basically did everything they could to keep from admitting that smoking caused cancer—and that they knew it.

Even though the federal government brought suit against Philip Morris, and ultimately won, the whole case was very disillusioning for me. Everyone knew that smoking caused cancer, but the government hadn't cared enough to do anything about it until now. And after the case was tried, the verdict was handed down, and all the appeals were considered, all that Philip Morris received was a slap on the wrist. They never had to pay any financial penalty for their wrongdoing. Admitting that they had known was the worst thing that happened to the company.

It was the final straw for me. Between the government's inaction—even corruption—and my work on immigration cases, I came away with an ugly feeling that not only was I not doing anything to help anyone, but that I was actually part of the problem.

I resigned not long after that case.

I had no job lined up. I had no plan for what I was going to do next. I just knew I couldn't stay there another day. The way I'd felt in that performance review meeting, having her look at me and tell me she controlled my livelihood, realizing what she saw when she looked at me—I'd felt that way all my life. I might feel I was becoming the real Tasha, and that I was gaining recognition for my work, but that experience rooted me in the reality that

I was still, in the eyes of many, overlooked. Taken for granted. Underestimated.

A Girl on Fire

When people found out I'd quit my job, they asked me if I was crazy. I was quitting a good-paying, stable government job, and I had nothing lined up? Not even a plan?

That's right, I told them. I didn't mind if they thought I was crazy, because I was used to it. I was used to being misunderstood, dismissed. All those negatives I've talked about in other chapters, being left behind and overlooked, feeling lonely because I was left alone, they'd made me strong. It was easy to ignore the doubters. I never had to ask them for anything.

I should have felt anxious, or scared, or desperate. In fact, I felt just the opposite. I never felt lost, never concerned. I felt *determined*. I was excited, eager, motivated. I was a girl on fire. Because I knew now what I was capable of.

The people around me, my real friends, could see it. I remember walking around the office sharing the news with the people that I was close to, and they could see it. I had something great to do, they told me.

Quitting that job was freeing. It was an escape from work that didn't make me feel good about what I was doing. But it was also more than that. Here I was taking the next step in my development.

I told myself, I've got to figure this out on my own without relying on anybody. That was my next step—I put all the burden on me. I just knew that I had to make a plan and execute it, to build something of my own so that my children never felt the way I had in that performance review, hearing someone tell me they could take my livelihood away with the flip of a switch or the stroke of a pen.

Even when I moved my kids and myself in with relatives for two days, and even when I qualified for public housing, I was never worried. People don't believe me when I say that, but it's true. I just knew I was going to build something great. Not just for me, but for my children. My goal wasn't to get by, it was to build an intergenerational legacy for myself *and* my children.

In the early days after quitting my job, I had to go on welfare. I had to use food stamps to feed myself and my children. There are some people who look down on welfare recipients, or attach a stigma to taking food stamps. Not me. I saw it as a government program that I had been paying into all the years I was working, and now that I was in transition and needed a temporary fix, I was going to use this program. There's absolutely nothing to be ashamed of.

And the aid that support provided me was immeasurable. Getting help with day care, for example, was an enormous help. I can't imagine being a single mother, trying to get a business off the ground, without that kind of support. (When I look back on the early years of my business, I can't even imagine how I did it, but that's another story!)

Things were hard financially, but that only drove me harder. Again, it didn't make me hopeless or desperate, it made me *determined*. That's who I'd always been, but it took a great challenge, that weight I put on myself, to really focus all that energy and willpower, to channel it into something great.

Starting at the Front Desk

My business developed from a temporary position that I took shortly after quitting my federal government position. I was brought on as a receptionist for a moving company. After my experience in government, moving up the ranks, you might think that working as a receptionist would feel like a step down. I didn't view it that way. This was the first step toward a new life, one where I was in control.

I was also entering an entirely new field. Here were new co-workers to meet. Working the front desk, answering phones in this new environment, with new things to learn, drove me. My self-esteem was high already, but it kept growing even as I took what many people would consider a big step back.

I've always loved to learn on the job: to get to know everything about a department or company, to get to know the people, to understand how all these people work together. Very quickly in that receptionist job, I got a good feel for how the moving company operated. I thought to myself, "I can do this—I could run a business like this." I saw the actual movers the company hired, bringing them on board on a contract basis, and I thought, "If I were doing this, I could hire my nephew or my cousin."

I kept my head down and continued to learn everything I could while I was at work. When I got home in the evening, I kept right on learning, reading everything I could find about how to start a business. I found a business plan online and I took it and ran with it. (I'm still running with it: more than twelve years later, I'm still using that original business plan. If it's not broke, why fix it?)

The result is that the time between my quitting my government job and jumping into my own venture as my own boss was less than a year.

When I was finally ready to make the leap into my own business, I did it the safest and smartest way I could think of: I returned to that same moving company as a consultant. The people there had seen me work, and even if I was "only" a receptionist, they knew I possessed the skill, knowledge, and drive to succeed as an extra project manager, working alongside their in-house staff on coordinating all the different aspects of a move. With my experience as a paralegal, plus all I'd learned about the company and the industry from my time as a receptionist, I was a smart pick to come in and help the company from my first day.

It was a smooth transition. At first, I could feel them looking at me differently, and I'm sure some of them wondered about trusting their former receptionist to coordinate all the many parts of a move. But it didn't take long before I proved myself. I hit the ground running with that first job, and I loved every minute of it. If I had to say what was the most different, the most empowering, the most *exciting* about that first job, it's simple: Being in charge!

That first big job was truly big: my team and I moved the Gaylord National Harbor Hotel. We were responsible for two thousand guest rooms, eight primary food service entrees, a nightclub, meeting rooms, a convention center, and an exhibit area. It was not just a big job, it was a big boost to my young company, and I describe it in detail in the next chapter.

On My Way

From there, I was on my way. It was never easy—as a single mother, it was exhausting, and frustrating, and there was always one more detail to take care of—but I enjoyed doing something that sparked my passion, that I knew I was good at, and that I could use to help others.

Looking back, there's so much I didn't know. I was my own accountant, my own hiring manager, my own marketing director. If I had it all to do over again, I'd find a partner to shoulder some of the workload. Yet on the other hand, by handling every aspect of the business myself I learned a great deal very quickly.

The process of moving an office is very complicated and there are endless details to keep track of. So I've always kept my business itself as simple as I could, first and foremost by keeping overhead low. In the beginning, I worked as a subcontractor for the company where I'd been a receptionist, but in more recent years I've been the prime contractor on a number of very large contracts with the federal government, working with agencies like the Federal Bureau of Investigation, the Centers for Disease Control, the United States Department of Agriculture, and the GSA.

Even as my career evolved and I became a prime contractor, I've stuck with my original business approach of keeping it simple. I use others' equipment and vehicles, and I hire movers on a contract basis, hiring them for each job, as needed. When the company bought a dump truck this past year, that was the first piece of big equipment we've ever purchased.

Nearly everything I've learned about how to run a business, I've learned on the job, picking things up as I go and learning from my own mistakes. Especially in the early days, I had to be resourceful, since my resources were strictly limited. I'm very proud that in all the years of running my business, I've never missed making payroll, and I've always performed—and often outperformed—the contracts I've signed with clients.

One of the things I'm most proud of is how my reputation has grown and spread. Early on, I learned the importance of little things, those extra touches that can make the difference between a mediocre business, one that gets by or fails, and a successful business that thrives and continues to grow, year over year.

When people talk about my business, they say that my team and I don't just come in and move boxes from Point A to Point B. They say that my experience as a federal employee means I know which hoops to jump through, which forms to obtain, who to invoice, and all the thousand ways to operate within the complicated federal government systems. When a company hires me, I take that burden off their shoulders.

People who've hired me know that my staff and I begin working weeks before the actual move, and the job doesn't end when the new office has been set up. For each client, I prepare a booklet of information on their new neighborhood: Here's the nearest dry cleaner, the post office is 0.2 miles away, here are some restaurants in the area. It's all come from looking at my own experience as a federal employee and from listening to my clients over years of doing this work. Giving my clients a little something extra isn't just a bonus, or a nice touch—it's at the center of the way I approach my business.

A Mentor

As much as I accomplished on my own over the course of this journey, I didn't get where I am without some help and guidance along the way. One of the biggest boosts to my business came from Shirley Blair, founder of Blair Temporaries and Staffing, Inc., based in nearby Silver Spring, Maryland.

When her company was selected as just one of three staffing agencies to participate in a $50 million contract with Bell South, Ms. Blair did something incredible. She went around the country, finding women like me who owned their own businesses, and subcontracted some of that Bell South contract to me and to women business owners like me. Coming at a critical time in the life of my young company, to have that business—and the vote of confidence that came with it—was an incredible boost.

Since then, she has been my mentor, and I've sought out her advice many times. She even calls me her godchild. As much as her help and guidance have helped me, her example has inspired me just as much. The impact she made by reaching out and involving others is hard to overestimate. She found small businesses and guided them. It's something that's helped drive me, and been an inspiration when I've had the opportunity to mentor others who are just getting started with their own businesses.

Reflections on the Journey

The whole experience of starting my own business from nothing, with no plan and no resources, has been incredibly rewarding, for so many reasons.

If there's a downturn in the economy, or a government spending freeze, we might go through a slow time, and I might have to hire fewer movers as contracted laborers, but I know we'll survive. My family's financial well-being is secure because I'm the one in control of it.

Since those very few times that I stayed with relatives, everyone has always come to live with me, whether it's family members or friends who look to "Aunt Tasha" for support. That's something I've always been proud of.

And it makes me proud when my daughter tells me about her friends comparing details of their tough childhoods and how they had to go without. She told me, "I had to be honest and say, 'I never experienced that.'" That was the biggest compliment my kids could pay me, to say that they never wanted for anything, they never felt hunger or cold, they always knew they'd have a roof over their heads.

Giving my children the opportunity to take control of their own destinies is something that I'll always be proud of, because no one can ever take from them the skills and confidence they've developed from being part of the business. I can give them a comfortable life, I can give them money, but best of all is to give them the tools to do it all on their own. That's a true intergenerational legacy.

As my employees, it's been incredible to see my children grow and flourish in their roles, to the point that I have the luxury of being hands off and motivating them to start their own businesses. To watch them take the talents and the self-confidence that they've built up, working for me, and apply that to their own businesses has made me so incredibly proud of them.

The satisfaction of hiring good people to work for me, regardless of whether they have a felony on their record, a college degree, or a high school diploma, is something that has never gotten old, that never fails to make me feel good about the way I conduct my business. To take someone who wants a chance to make an honest day's work and give them that chance to provide for their family is one of the great pleasures of the business I've built.

The men and women I hire are grateful for the chance to work, but one of the first things I tell them is, "I'm giving you your raise, but it's your job to keep it." I don't fire anyone, I tell my workers—they fire themselves by failing to do the job.

It all depends on what you put into the work, I tell them. It's how I still approach my own role as the head of the company, and the standard I still hold myself to.

That feeling of standing behind my work, going home tired but proud of what I've done, is exactly what I was searching for when I decided to leave my government job and bet on myself.

Chapter Seven

Entrepreneurship

I f you believe in yourself, you're not rolling the dice or taking your chances. It's not a bet if you're confident that you're going to succeed. Going out on my own never felt like a bet to me because I knew what I was capable of and I knew that if I worked hard, planned ahead, and handled things the right way, "betting" on myself wasn't as big a risk as some people might think.

Look at my first big job as a business owner. It was at the Gaylord National Harbor Hotel in Maryland. If the idea of moving an entire hotel doesn't give you a sense of how big this job was, consider that the Gaylord had five thousand hotel rooms *and* a convention center, a nightclub, and eight kitchens. If you imagine how much furniture is in a single hotel room, not to mention the tables and equipment in the convention center, you'll begin to have an idea of what an enormous undertaking this was.

We did an excellent job. I'm not just saying that: the hotel's management told us this, and the partners my company worked with on the move told us. Much more importantly, these people told other people. Word spread. Soon, we had a contract to help the Department of Transportation move their offices.

So you see what I mean when I say that I never felt I was taking a big chance on myself. If I did what I was supposed to, hired the people I wanted to hire, and we all stuck to the plan, great things would happen. And that's exactly what did happen. And once the word got around that TBS Facility Services had done such an incredible job on such a difficult job, prospective clients came calling.

To this day, more than twelve years after beginning the business, I've only bid competitively for jobs *twice*. That's extremely unusual. Putting together bids to compete for jobs is a major part of many companies' business. TBS has been fortunate enough to have our clients come to us. We've made our own "luck" by consistently going beyond our clients' expectations and earning the kind of word of mouth that has helped the company flourish.

My First Big Job

The job moving the Gaylord National Harbor Hotel required companies to enter bids. The winning bid was submitted by the company that I had worked for—first as a temporary receptionist and then as a consultant. To win the bid, they used my resume, showing my qualifications from having managed a number of jobs for the company.

But not so fast. One of the companies that had submitted a bid protested, because the terms of the request for bids had stated that the job must go to a small company. My former employer— let's call them Company A—had to work out a compromise, bringing in Company B as the primary contractor working on this contract. They would then subcontract moving services to Company B, which would bring me on as a project manager, working as an employee.

No, no, no. I told them I was finished working as an employee. But they could bring my company on as a subcontractor. To be honest, I think they were a little surprised that I knew I could do that. But I'd done my homework. In any event, they agreed, and TBS Facility Services, Inc., was hired for the job.

Because of my experience and because I knew contracts well enough to understand what was in the deal with the State of Maryland, I went to the first planning meeting knowing what kind of leverage I had. I knew how many trucks and laborers were needed for the job. I knew that the team needed twenty-five laborers, for example. And I said that fifteen of those laborers had to be from TBS. When they argued, I told them that if they didn't let TBS provide fifteen of the laborers, we'd pull out of the contract.

They agreed that TBS would provide the bulk of the laborers. I was so excited—here I was finally living my dream of being able to provide opportunities to friends, family, and neighbors.

I was excited until I got home, that is. Where was I supposed to get fifteen laborers?

I at least knew where five of them would come from. I would hire my actual nephew and four of his friends, who'd become like nephews to me. I started going around looking for all the able-bodied men I knew. I felt like Oprah, telling people, "You get a job and you get a job." It was exactly what I had set out to do and it was an incredible feeling.

My team went in wearing Company A's T-shirts. It was a little bittersweet for me: here we were, getting our first big break with a truly enormous and challenging job, undertaken by the crew I'd personally selected—and it wasn't my name on the back of those shirts. But honestly, I couldn't complain, because we were getting this big break— and because there were a million details to take care of during the move.

It was intense. We worked six days a week, always ten-to-twelve-hour days. The entire job took six months. Those were some of the most stressful days of my life. But that was exactly how I started the business—getting thrown into the fire—so why shouldn't my first job be the same way? I always tell people, I was on fire because I was thrown into the fire.

With a job that big, there was no ignoring the fact that I was in charge of my own team. Whereas I'd worked as a consultant on previous jobs, during the Gaylord move I can remember thinking, "Oh, wow, I'm a company." It felt like I was really getting a foothold in the business.

The long and short of it is, that job is where TBS was truly born.

My Team

One of the most gratifying parts of that first big job was that I got to personally choose people I wanted to hire on the project. That was the start of a tradition I've been very proud to continue throughout the more than twelve years that the business has been running. I've always reached back to the community, to friends and family.

It's been one of the most satisfying aspects of my life as a business owner, both personally and professionally, to offer employment to so many men and women, giving them the opportunity to provide for themselves and their families. On that first job, I was able to provide employment to a number of my nephews, and to some

young men who became my nephews. (They call me "Aunt Ta.")
Just as significantly, I was able to offer work to young men who'd
just returned from being incarcerated. These were young men I
knew from the neighborhood, whose families I'd grown up with.
Where many other employers were passing them by for work, I
didn't hesitate to bring them on to my team.

Apart from facing discrimination due to possible criminal
records, many of the men in my neighborhood faced hardships due
to factors such as the high unemployment rate. The moving jobs
that I hire for don't require a degree or even a high level of work
experience: we use a color and numerical code to keep everything
in order, so I can hire these men and women with confidence that
they'll do a good job.

Hiring from the community has been a way to help out since
that very first big job, and the desire to provide the opportunity
to work remains at the forefront of TBS's philosophy to this day.

Another great pleasure during my professional career has
been to watch some of the people I've hired as movers evolve to
bigger things. Even among the team I assembled for that Gaylord
job, there are college graduates, business owners, and even two
ministers! I have no doubt that for at least some of them, working
for TBS was the chance they needed to get to that next level in
life. And many of these former employees are actively "paying it
forward" by hiring others who may be in circumstances similar
to themselves at one point. If I ever need affirmation, or to find a
reason to feel good about this business that I've built, I don't have
to look beyond this cycle and how it continues to provide help
and opportunities.

Word of Mouth

Not long after the Gaylord move, the Department of Transportation contacted me. They were moving into a new building and wanted my company to handle the move.

This time, I made sure that my team had my T-shirts on. And we had already taken a step forward from the Gaylord National Harbor Hotel job: We moved 5,500 federal employees into a new ten-story, 1.2-million-square-feet office building. We took care of all the Department's computers, disconnecting them and reconnecting them at the new building.

That early job was like a seed for the company—we now specialize in computer moves. In 2017, we were awarded the contract at the General Services Administration to move all the computers, boxes, and furniture of the Obama Administration to make room for the incoming presidential administration. Proudly, I subcontracted out the computer setup to Dynamic V Solutions (my nephew's company).

The Department of Transportation was so pleased with the job we did, they offered us a five-year contract. TBS Facilities employees set up an office in a Department of Transportation building, where they're on call during business hours to move anything that needs to be moved within the Department. I negotiated those employees' salaries with the government, and got them to pay for top-secret clearance training as well as information technology training. My nephew was one of the employees we placed at the Department of Transportation and we both realized this was a golden opportunity for him to learn everything he could about computers with all his schooling paid for. Ultimately, he took that training and ended up working as the lead on a service server team managing twenty federal employees within the Department of Justice. Today he runs his own technology firm.

The Secret of My Success

Just recently, I made a series of Facebook Live videos, talking with anyone who wanted to watch, answering all their questions. I'm happy to help other people and share my experience. I love mentoring young entrepreneurs and sharing my passion. My soul is invested in this business, and I love what I do. If I can help someone by answering questions about the right kind of paperwork to file, or where to look to find government contracts, I'm happy to do it.

Some businesspeople hide their secrets. Not me. I'll tell anyone who listens that I've gotten to where I am by keeping overhead low—until just recently, TBS didn't have its own offices, and we just purchased our first dump truck—and by hiring workers on a contract basis (a 1099 tax form) instead of full-time (a W-2 form). I hope those ideas will help someone.

And anyway, those things aren't my *real* secret. The actual secret of my success is that I have a passion for this business, for creating something of my own and—even more than that—for creating an intergenerational legacy.

One of the main lessons from my experience is that there is no set of instructions that will guide you toward whatever goal you have in mind. I've run into people with graduate degrees in business who can't figure out how to start a business, and in twelve years at the head of TBS I've seen many businesses come and go. Executing, delivering on your promises, giving the client what they want and even anticipating their needs, going that extra mile: those are my business secrets, and they're all more easily said than done.

If you want to do something, you just have to do it. I didn't know the world of moving all that well when I got into the business—I just had a few contacts and knew how to manage a team. I didn't have anyone to mentor me one-on-one, walking me through everything step by step. As I've said, my business plan came off the internet (and I still haven't updated it since 2009!).

I was thrown into the fire and because of that I learned quickly. That's what made me a raging bull. That's what I tell people when they want to know my secret. Figuring it out myself has always been my secret.

"You have to be hungry." I'm trying to be a legacy, and that makes me hungry.

What Entrepreneurship Means to Me

When people remember me, I want them to say, "One thing about Tasha, she always reached back to help others." I want them to remember that I looked back at where I came from and I reached my hand out to help others up.

I want to inspire people.

If I could, I would save the world. When I share my story as an entrepreneur, I'm not trying to hold on to my secrets. What I would love, the reason I share my story, is that someone who's been creating a product or doing a service will think to themselves, "Maybe I could start a business." That's what entrepreneurship means to me: starting something for yourself—and for me, it means inspiring others to start something for themselves.

Starting and running your own business is about as hard a job as there is. There are so many ups and downs, so many days when you work from dawn until way past dusk and go to sleep with your work only half done. I've been in business over a dozen years and it's only been within the last few years that I've been able to hire someone else to do my taxes, and to hand off some of my duties to my children. For the rest of that time, I was everything: hiring manager, accountant, marketing person, and so on—if there was a job to be done, I was either the one doing it or I'd hired the people taking care of it.

But this idea of entrepreneurship is wrong in spirit, too. Entrepreneurship isn't about having millions of dollars. It's about paying things forward. Helping your community.

It's about teaching your children how to fish instead of bringing home the fish. It's about giving them the skills and confidence to start their own ventures and to know that they can succeed. Just as important, it's about knowing that if they don't succeed, they can turn around and try again, or move on to the next thing and try again.

I want to continue to plant seeds so I'll never die.

Entrepreneurship is even bigger than teaching your children to fish, though. It's about creating an intergenerational legacy. My children, if and when they have children of their own, can teach those kids how to create something of their own.

I don't do this for myself alone. I do this for the legacy that I leave behind, so they can do it for themselves. Right now, I'm as proud as I can be of my two children and the work they do for my company. But I'm just as proud of the businesses they've started on their own. That's what tells me that my own entrepreneurship, and the things I've tried to teach them, are having an effect. I love working with them, but I couldn't be more excited for the day that they decide to step out on their own and leave TBS behind.

Entrepreneurship is about sweat equity. It's about integrity. It's about community. Entrepreneurship as I approach and practice it isn't selfish—quite the opposite. It's about looking back and pulling others up behind me. It's for my own family, and it's for the people around me, my neighbors and friends.

Small businesses are truly what make America great. The reason isn't because so many people become millionaires, or drive around in BMWs and Mercedes-Benzes. Creating jobs, building sweat equity, starting a legacy, all are the things that make this country great.

When people think about entrepreneurship, they picture *The Jeffersons*: a rich family that moved away from all their old friends once they made it big. But entrepreneurship is really more like *Sanford and Son*: they stayed right where they were, rooted in their community. Fred Sanford's business was junk, but he was a business owner, just as much as George Jefferson.

What Success Means to Me

When someone asks me the secret to my success, I have to ask them how they define success. For a lot of entrepreneurs, the answer involves money. That's never what it's been about for me.

Success to me is seeing my children be successful independent of what I've done for them financially. It's seeing them learn from what I did: the sacrifices, the trial and error, the highs and lows.

Both of my children work for the company, but just as important, they both have businesses of their own. It's not about creating a company so that they will always have a job, or so that, if they have children of their own, those children will have jobs someday.

My goal as an entrepreneur is not to provide my children and grandchildren with jobs in TBS Facilities, LLC.

There's nothing wrong with the goal many entrepreneurs start out with: starting a family business so that their children and grandchildren will always have a job waiting for them. That's very much how I thought about TBS when I started out: a business that my children could one day help run.

But as the business has grown, as I've grown, and as my sense of what entrepreneurship can be has grown, my goals for myself and my children—and their children—have changed.

I've tried to model this for my children, how much better it feels having a hard day working for myself and my family than a hard day working for somebody else. It's a whole different feeling, and there's no comparison. Even a hard day working to build that intergenerational legacy feels better than an average day working for somebody else.

Success to me is no longer going onto job sites, because my children have learned the business so well that I don't have any worries about one of them supervising a move.

Success is financial comfort. For too many entrepreneurs, that's the *only* measure of success. But it certainly is part of success. I own two homes, and just added a pool to one of them. I can take a nice vacation when I want to. There's nothing wrong with enjoying the comforts that come from working hard. The problem is when that's the only reason you're working hard.

Success to me is helping others and getting them to a position where they can succeed no matter what I do, no matter what happens with TBS.

I bet on me. Success to me is not watching my children collect on that bet—it's watching them gain the confidence and skills to bet on themselves and win.

My success is seeing their success.

Chapter Eight

Helping Family and Defining Success

As I mentioned in the last chapter, success has never been about money for me.

The only value of money, as far as I'm concerned, is in the comfort and security it can provide. That's what I really wanted, for myself and my family, when I first started my own business. It wasn't about buying an expensive car—it was about having enough money to put gas in the tank, or to get my car fixed if it should break down.

As I've evolved as an entrepreneur, as a leader, and as a parent, I've extended that philosophy. It's not about being able to fix *my* car if it should break down or get a flat tire. It's about helping others so that they can take care of themselves, no matter what comes their way.

For me, helping family is the definition of success. Putting people in position to better their lives: that's not just how I define success, it's why I strive to succeed. If I can't help others through my position, what good is it? And what good am I doing?

My Nephew

Take the example of my nephew. While there are many young men who call me Aunt Tasha (or Aunt Tay, or some other version of my name), the truth is I only have one nephew, my sister's son.

And although he is my nephew, he's as close to me as if he were a son. I've helped raise him, and he's spent nearly as much time hanging around my house as if he were my actual son. I've seen him grow from a little baby to an incredible, independent, ambitious young man with a family of his own.

When I started my company and we landed our first big job, at the Gaylord National Harbor Hotel, my nephew was among the first people I hired.

At that time, he was a very different person from the man he is today. At seventeen years old, my nephew was not very motivated, like many young men his age. He'd hang around my house for hours, and seemed to think that I was going to take care of him and let him be lazy.

Hiring him for that first job was my way of saying, "No, you will not do that around me." It was also my way of reaching out to him, showing him that I wanted and expected better from him.

I hired him as a laborer. He was excited about the chance to make money, especially because it was a big job. But he wasn't thinking beyond that. He wasn't thinking about a career, or ways he could take this little opportunity and turn it into a big opportunity.

But once he got on that first job site, something happened. It was like a switch flipped inside him. My nephew threw himself into the work. He hustled, he demonstrated a great work ethic and attitude, and he was eager to learn everything he could. Although I'd told him what I expected of him, and he knew how important that first big job was to the company, I was inspired by how completely he threw himself into the work.

Right from day one, he was a professional: he was always on time, and he showed up ready and eager to work. And he wanted to learn everything.

He became so immersed in the work, when he would go off shift, he'd find a place at the work site to hide and take a nap so that he could come back and pick up a second shift.

As proud as I was of his work ethic on that first job, it was TBS's second job, with the Department of Transportation (DOT), where my nephew really started down the path that he continues to walk today.

That was when he first came in contact with the world of information technology (IT). As I've mentioned, the DOT job involved disconnecting computer equipment so that it could be reconnected after we'd moved everything. The reconnecting was not in our purview. A team would follow behind us, reconnecting everything and turning all the computers on, making sure that everything was connected and working properly.

I told my nephew, "Make sure you learn something about what they're doing."

My purpose in telling him this was twofold. First, I hoped that eventually TBS could offer the services that second team was providing, offering clients a truly full-service experience. Second, I wanted my nephew to have the knowledge that would give him options in his career.

Now, I could hardly tell you what my nephew learned. Whenever he tries to explain his IT work to me, most of it goes over my head. But he definitely learned something on that job, and from all the other work TBS did at the DOT after they signed us to a long-term contract there. I think already, at just eighteen or so years of age, he sensed that being exposed to IT and to other IT professionals was an incredible opportunity, and he grabbed hold of it.

Two years ago, he resigned his position to form his own IT company. Today, he has major federal contracts, providing consulting services on government projects.

Does that sound like anyone else's story? As I said, I don't understand half of the technical things he does. I certainly didn't teach him any of that end of things. But I believe that when it comes to being an entrepreneur, and the value of working for himself, he learned a great deal from his Aunt Tasha. Some of it I told him, but most of it he picked up from working close by me and paying attention.

He wanted to be able to provide for his family, including his mother, siblings, and grandmother. He wanted to employ others. He wanted to run the show, just like his aunt did.

And how did he do it all? By learning as he went, just like I did. I can honestly say that most of what he's accomplished he's done by his own ambition and drive. As I said before, you can't teach motivation or the will to succeed.

Today, my nephew is married with a family. He just recently turned thirty and is a major player in the D.C. area in the world of IT.

When my nephew walked onto that first job site, he never could have imagined that it would lead him to his flourishing career. As far as he knew, this was just a quick job that would put some money in his pocket. But something just clicked, and it turned on a side of him I don't think he even realized he had: the go-getter, the motivated and driven young man who today is excited to go to work each morning and continues to learn all he can about the world around him, constantly seeking out ways to apply it to his own business.

He didn't wait for life to happen. He made life happen. And he's still doing that.

Seeing that as an aunt, I couldn't be prouder. His success is my success.

My Other "Nephews"

My nephew's success inspires me. Not just because I feel good about giving him that first opportunity, that encouragement to learn and ask questions, to soak up all the information he could.

There are a lot of young men who work for me who also call me "Aunt Tasha." And even outside the company, as I go about my day-to-day life, I meet a lot of young black men who remind me of my nephew when he was seventeen years old. They don't have a clear direction in life. They can't see the greatness in themselves.

But I can. Sometimes I think I believe in these young men more than they believe in themselves.

Because of that, I treat the young men on my job sites the same way I treated my nephew. I treat each and every one of them as if they were capable of going on to great things: running their own businesses, college, raising families of their own. It may be something entirely different, something that neither I nor they can even imagine. And I don't know how they're going to get there. I just know that they are capable of achieving it.

When I see one of these young men who is not living up to his potential, I tell him, "You should be doing more than you are doing now."

Or I'll say, "You're great but you could be greater."

I want to challenge someone, whether it's someone in my family, my community, or someone who works for me. But I'm not going to tear them down. I want to build them up—but I also want them to know that they could be doing something greater, something more meaningful with their lives.

My Son

When I look at my nephew's success, I see someone who learned from TBS and the opportunities that came with working for the company. For him, things just clicked.

With my son, it wasn't like that at all. He started on those same first jobs as my nephew, but it didn't grab him the way it did my nephew. He worked for the company for a few years, but he wasn't quite ready.

At the time, he had finished high school and, like many mothers and sons, we would occasionally battle over what he was going to do next. "You don't have to go to college," I told him, "but you have to do something."

Working for the company was one of the jobs he held, but as I said, it didn't inspire him at that time the way it did my nephew.

My son made some bad choices at this time in his life. He was incarcerated and spent three years in prison. It broke my heart to see him go through this process, and to stand in the courtroom on the day of his sentencing. On the day that he went into prison to serve his sentence, I wrote my son a poem expressing everything I was feeling: I wrote this poem one year later after his incarceration.

You are my son, a part of me, and that will never change,
No matter what you do in life my love will still remain.

I held you as a baby and I looked into your face
And I knew then, no other one could ever take your place.

I knew then as I held you, you would grow to be a man
And anything you did in life I'd try to understand.

I knew you would make choices and would follow your own heart,
I only prayed that in your life I'd always have a part.

I know some things you do in life would give me so much pride
But also realize some things would tear me up inside.

I only want the best for you and want you to succeed
And want you to find happiness with everything you need.

I can only guide and give you a helping hand,
You will choose the path to take now that you are a man.

Along the road that you will choose, whatever that may be,
Just remember this, my son: that you can count on me.

I will not try to push you to live life in my own stride,
I only promise I will love you and stand by your side.

I know that you will make mistakes and life is full of them,
But realize my love for you will not let me condemn.

I know this life's not perfect and we do the best we can,
Just realize I love you and I'll always understand.

I knew one day you would grow up and you would leave my nest,
I will do what I can for you and let GOD do the rest.

I have held you in my arms and done the best I can,
I know that God will hold you now that you're a man.

Just remember in my heart you are a special one,
And I will always proudly tell the world, "Yes, he is my son!"

Reading that poem now brings back all the mixed-up feelings I felt from the time of his arrest through the trial and sentencing, to those long three years when he was away. To this day, that period of my life was one of the most difficult I've ever gone through, and that's because it affected not just me but my family.

And yet if you know anything about me by now, you know that I always look for the positive in any experience or situation, even if—*especially if*—those experiences are negative.

Looking back on that time now, I truly believed that his time in prison saved my son's life. It forced him to sit down and think about the decisions he was making. God had to have a talk with him. It made my son realize that he's adult enough to make decisions on his own, and that there's a great responsibility that comes with that.

He entered prison a lost and troubled boy and he emerged a man. Today he is focused, determined, and motivated. Whenever we talk about it (which is very seldom, if ever—it's in our past), he agrees that on the day he left prison he came out with a spirit of determination to make something happen for himself, not waiting on life and not expecting anything from anybody else. I'll describe his entrepreneurship more in a later chapter, but I don't think he would have done the things he has done if he had never gone to prison and been forced to slow down, sit with himself, and have that talk with God.

Even after his incarceration, I've never pushed my son to work with me at TBS. I just let him know that whatever he decided he wanted, ultimately, I'd be behind him 100 percent.

But as I said earlier, helping my family, paving the way to their success, is about giving them the tools to make their own way—not making sure they have a job in the family business whenever they want one. I truly mean that, and it starts with my own children.

For right now, it so happens that my son has a real passion for the business. He may be a later bloomer than my nephew, but that doesn't matter a bit. He's every bit as driven, focused, and serious about doing the job. He wants to be there, and he wants to lead within TBS.

He's so committed, and so good at the job, over the last three years, I've rarely ever had to go to a job site because I know my son will be there, and I trust his judgment. His leadership, hard work, and commitment to TBS have been a godsend these past few years, and I'm deeply thankful for my son's contributions. It makes me incredibly proud to see him thriving in this role.

After almost a decade of taking care of every single detail and doing every job there was to do at TBS, it's incredibly liberating to know that I can leave daily operations in my son's control.

He knows the quality we aspire to, and the level of service we expect. I don't have to hold his hand or look over his shoulder. I give him the freedom to do things however he sees fit, provided he meets those standards of quality and service. He manages the team his way, and he employs the people he needs to get the job done right.

At the same time that he is thriving in his role at TBS, my son has other ambitions. He has big plans for himself. He owns his own clothing company.

It's all part of his larger goal to build something for himself. And I know there's going to come a day when one of his other ventures begins to take off, and he can no longer do it on the side. He'll have to quit TBS and leave the company to pursue his dreams.

And you know what? On that day, I won't be the least bit sad. I'll be happy for my son, and I'll be rooting for him, because watching him find success in something he's passionate about, that he wants to pursue—well, that's my success. That's exactly what I want to be doing.

My Daughter

My daughter is every bit as inspiring to me as my son. She has been invaluable to me practically from the beginning of TBS, assisting me in preparing for the Gaylord project. She has been helping to support the business since she was sixteen, and over that time she has only become more knowledgeable about the inner workings of the business. Although she's doing a phenomenal job as my son's second-in-command, I know that working for TBS isn't her ultimate life goal.

She's a talented cook, going back to the days when she would help her mother, grandmother, and her aunts on her father's side in the kitchen. As a high school student she developed a real love for being around food, often staying late to help her school's culinary arts program prepare snacks for parent-teacher conferences. Twice during her high school career she won the school's award for best culinary arts student.

Not only that, but for the past several years she has run her own wholesale jewelry line, buying and selling pieces of jewelry through a business called Bria's Boutique. I helped her to set it up, but since then it has been her passion and vision that have driven the business.

My daughter inspires me not only through her culinary skill or her taste in jewelry, though. I am continually impressed by her ambition and her ability to strategize and figure out ways that she can create opportunities for herself.

After years of working in restaurants around the D.C. area, she had the knowledge, skill, and resume to create her own venture. She founded a business where she will come out to a person's house and cook for them for the night. It may be a husband and wife who want to have a date night at home, or it may be a small party.

Part of her strategy in growing the business is to take occasional catering jobs. She worked in a kitchen as a way to gain experience and valuable exposure.

But she shares my dislike of working for other people, unless it is for someone in the family. Her approach is to juggle jobs when she needs them, maintaining the flexibility to keep her own business ventures going full speed ahead.

That desire not to get bogged down or trapped is one reason she's so intent on building her own empire. From her experience with TBS, she's seen how people get rooted in jobs, especially jobs with the federal government. Get a degree, get a job, and suddenly you look up and twenty years have passed. That's not for my daughter. She wants to be the boss, just like her mother.

While she keeps all this going, she also finds the time to help me out when I need a hand with TBS jobs, big and small. She's an enormous help to me, but she also knows that I don't want her to get caught up in being a TBS employee. When one of my daughter's businesses takes off, and she can't find the time to help out with the logistics of a big move, I'll celebrate right along with her.

In the meantime, I'm helping her get there. If she has a question about contracts or certifications, I'm happy to go through it with her, step by step. And I believe that both my children have been able to apply the skills they've learned from working at TBS in pursuit of their own businesses.

But what both my children have told me is that it's not what they've learned from me as their boss that's inspired them and made them on fire to go out and create their own businesses, their own source of income and security.

It's what they've seen and learned from me as their mother.

For my daughter, she was about twelve years old when I went out on my own. She was old enough to understand what was happening and to hear all those people telling me I was crazy, that I'd never make it, that I couldn't do what I was doing. And then she watched as I got my first certifications, learned how to bid on my first jobs, and won those first contracts.

She was also old enough to understand what I was talking about when I said that I didn't want to work for anybody anymore. When she was old enough to go and get jobs in kitchens around town, she did that, but I think that was always in the back of her mind: at the end of the day, you work for yourself. You take care of your own livelihood, and the best way of doing that is by becoming your own boss.

That wasn't just something I told my children. It was something I showed them, every day that I was working long hours to build up my business.

A Family of Entrepreneurs

Just recently, my children and I were sitting at the kitchen table, eating lunch together. It was a Thursday at noon.

In the middle of conversation, it struck me how blessed we are to be able to just sit down together, right in the middle of the workweek, and enjoy lunch.

What's even more blessed, I thought later, is that if I were to make that observation to my children, they wouldn't even see it as strange. It's all so natural to them.

This, too, is part of how I define success. To make owning their own businesses, working for themselves, so natural that they don't even realize how lucky they are.

I would worry if I felt my children took all this for granted. But I don't see that in them. They know how hard I worked to build the business, and from running their own businesses they know that going off on your own as an entrepreneur isn't the easiest path available. They know it takes hard work, perseverance, motivation, and commitment. I'm confident that they won't take business ownership for granted.

As I have become successful, it has been important to me to communicate my values and my ambitions to my children. Giving them not just the job or the material comfort to do what they want, but passing on that hustle, that sense of commitment and possibility.

You can't put a monetary value on the pleasure of watching your children succeed and do great things. That's winning in life.

Continuing a Legacy

Just as sweet as seeing my children succeed is recognizing how they're continuing the legacy that I've tried to start with them: reaching back and helping others.

As leaders at TBS, in their own businesses, and as partners in my nonprofit organization, they're hiring and helping community members, giving people the jobs they need to support their families and to make something of themselves.

That's something that I know inspires my children and makes them proud to work with TBS. They were both right there, watching as my nephew turned the opportunity I gave him into a career, and as my nephew, in turn, has helped others. Bria witnessed her brother's friends work for TBS. She's seen her brother come back changed, ready to build something for himself. She's seen young men who have been incarcerated take jobs with TBS and avoid having to go back to prison because of the work we've given them. And because of what that work represents: pride, independence, the ability to support themselves and their families.

Through our nonprofit organization, we're making a difference in the lives of those recently returned from prison, giving them the training and support they need to make that transition smoothly and successfully.

As an entrepreneur, you can create so much more than money. You can inspire. You can build up individuals. You can introduce hope and passion into people's lives. You can teach discipline, independence, enthusiasm, and pride. You can change a person's life forever and give them the ability to change others' lives as well.

That's what gives me purpose and passion in my life: feeling that my children's giving back is part of the legacy I helped create.

Watching my son, in particular, give back to the community is an inspiring and humbling sight. I'm so proud of him and of the fact that he was able to come home from incarceration and not only readjust, not only contribute to TBS's success, but take a real leadership role in the company and start his own business venture.

When I look at the continuation of my legacy, I know that this is why I was put here.

I know now that this is the reason I'm here on this earth. For all the times, as a young girl, that I wondered why I was even born, I have my answer when I see my children giving back to the people around them.

Now I know my why.

Chapter Nine

Parenting

Becoming a parent is the greatest gift given to me in this world. That doesn't mean it's always been easy, or fun—as a single mother raising two children, I'd be lying if I said it was ever easy. But watching my son and daughter grow up has been the greatest experience of my life. Their very lives are a blessing to me.

Parenting is the kind of job for which there is no practice. When I gave birth to my son at age twenty-three, I couldn't have known what to expect. I'm blessed that the father of both my children is my best friend to this day. Although we didn't succeed in marriage, we were great co-parents, and I always felt supported as a mother to my children.

As a parent, you give it your best shot and trust that God will make your children resilient enough that when you make mistakes, those errors don't cause your children harm or lead them to suffer.

Notice that I didn't say, "If you make mistakes." You try your best but caring for a child, whether it's a screaming infant at three in the morning, or a toddler who doesn't want to get dressed to leave the house, is an ever-changing experience. A child will find new ways to surprise and challenge you every day. And if you're sleep-deprived, frustrated, and running short on patience, you may not react to those challenges the way a parenting guidebook says you should.

That's true no matter who you are, and it goes double for single parents. For me, constantly working to build something to support myself and my child—not just for the next meal or the next week, but for the long term—the stress and strain were monumental.

My children and I were fortunate that their father stayed in their lives. That certainly isn't always the case for single parents. Not only that, but the children's father and his family provided tremendous support, emotionally and financially. Their side of the family was key to showing my children just how much family can mean to you, what a healthy family can look like when all the members care deeply about one another. Their side of the family worshipped together and they had an annual family gathering that was a joy to attend and to bring my children to each year.

Just as importantly, that side of the family was key to making sure I kept my children close to God. While faith has always been important to me, it's at the very center of that family's life, and it was from them that my children learned about faith and building a relationship with God.

When you raise your second child, you may feel that you have experienced everything and that nothing will surprise you. But of course you learn quickly that that isn't true. Especially in my case, the differences between my two children caught me off guard. You can't just reuse the clothes you dressed your first baby in, for starters. And the older my children grew, the more different they became.

All of that is beside the fact that now I had two little children I was in charge of, and that while I was doing that I had to go out and earn a steady paycheck and think about the future. Two children were a blessing, but they were also a complication. It was no longer just me who depended on the decisions I made and the money I brought home. Even with the support I had, the stakes were undeniably higher.

Of course I made mistakes. As my children grew older, sometimes I pushed too hard. Whether it was pushing them to study harder and earn better grades than what they were bringing home, or being respectful and obedient in the home, I know that at times I asked more of them than was right.

And at other times, I didn't push nearly hard enough. Maybe I was afraid of pushing too hard and alienating my children. Maybe I thought that they couldn't handle all that I wanted to put on their shoulders. (Now that they are older I can see clearly just how much they are capable of, and it is an awesome sight. They are resilient, intelligent, passionate, loving, and caring.)

Regardless, I made my fair share of mistakes as I raised my children. As they've grown into fine adults, trusted colleagues in the business, one of the most meaningful ways I've found to connect with them is by talking openly and honestly about nearly everything. That includes the simple, honest admission that their mother didn't always make the perfect, correct choice when they were growing up.

Your mother is human, I can tell them now. She owns up to her mistakes and—the most important thing about admitting your mistakes—she learns from them and tries to make them right. Especially with them now being part of the business, that openness now extends to talking through a problem, a business opportunity, a decision I need to make. Here are the pros and cons, or here's something I'm not sure of: what do you think?

It's one of the continuing blessings of having children. The older they get, the more honest we can be with each other, and the more we can treat one another not as mother and child but as peers, colleagues, and friends.

Balancing Business with Family

On one hand, having children when I went out on my own with TBS made everything more difficult. I had less time to dedicate to all of the details you have to take care of when you start a business. I definitely had less money to pour into the business than I would have had if I'd never had children.

Having two young children at the time also made everything trickier. Again, I'm so grateful that their father remained in the picture. He came to pick the children up every other weekend. His family, including the children's grandfather, also helped us immensely.

I was also able to obtain free day care from the Department of Social Services. This was truly a blessing. Not only did day care allow me to dedicate each day's focus to my work, but from the time they were about six weeks old, my children were in a structured and nurturing learning environment. This built a critical foundation for their education.

I also got a lot of support from the children's godmother and godfather. They loved and cared for the children like they were a part of their own families. They also provided financial support that made all the difference to me at that time in my life.

Looking back, I'm struck by the fact that all of my support came from outside my own family, whether it was from the family of the children's father or from government programs. I believe this has played a key role in developing my passion for helping the community. So many people just can't rely on family networks.

Together, all this support allowed me to focus on the task at hand and concentrate everything I had on building my business, networking, getting the TBS name out there.

On the other hand, my children are the reason I decided to start my own business. They are what fueled my passion to succeed, and it's impossible to separate being a mother from being a business owner, or looking at my decisions as a mother apart from my decisions as a business owner.

Having children helped me focus more on my life and what I wanted out of it. It made me wake up and ask myself hard questions about what my actual goals were, versus what other people expected of me.

The wonderful thing about having your children inspire you is that you can never forget that kind of inspiration or leave it behind. It's not a passing desire or motivation like when someone is hustling to make more money, earn a promotion and a fancy new title, or carry out a New Year's resolution.

As I've said, what I'm after is building a legacy. A business empire that offers financial stability but also a crucial stepping-stone that my children can use to launch their own business pursuits. When you're working toward that kind of goal, money and titles aren't enough motivation.

But looking in your children's faces and thinking about what their lives will be like, and the lives of their children—that's the kind of motivation that will keep you hustling, day in and day out.

I'd always find the time to call home from the office, or out on the job site, and make sure my children had all studied, or check that they were dressed and ready for school.

For a long time, everything in my life was focused on my business. But that doesn't mean I ever neglected or forgot about my children. Just the opposite: I found ways to be involved in their lives, to check in on them, to ask them how they were doing.

They were what inspired me and drove me forward, and if you could have peeled back the passion and intensity I brought to my business to discover what was *truly* driving me forward, it was them. It was always them.

That driving force continues to this day. I don't do anything without asking myself how it will impact my children. Does a decision create opportunities for my son and daughter? Will it make difficulties for them, or does it give them the flexibility not to be tied down by TBS business, free to break off and pursue their own ventures if that's what they need to do? There is no business decision that is *only* a business decision, because it all begins and ends with my family.

What's really special is that as my son and daughter have grown into intelligent, confident, and competent young people, I'm no longer making these decisions simply with them in mind. Nowadays, very often I make the decisions *with* them: if I'm thinking of a new initiative or debating whether to bid on a new job, I can bounce ideas off of them and get their perspectives.

After years of being at the center of what I did, and being the reason for it, today they're truly at the center of our business as decision makers and trusted partners.

Overcoming Negative Patterns

But my identity as a business owner is just one part of who I am. As a parent, I also bring my experiences, pleasurable and painful, into the way I raise my children.

When I had my son, I was no longer the quiet, forgotten little girl who spent so many summers inside, or lying on her belly in a hospital room. I'd been through a whole range of important experiences that gave me the confidence to know I had what it took to raise this child and provide him with all the safety and comfort he needed.

But that Tasha, lonely and overlooked, is still with me. She'll always be a part of me. And the little girl who never got the love she needed, whose father was never there even though he was always just a few miles from home—she has never left me completely, either.

So often the way we are treated dictates who we become. It would have been so natural to treat my children the way I was treated, the way I was loved.

But as I've detailed, my experiences being lonely and neglected strengthened me. I determined long ago that I don't have to settle for the way things are usually done, or do what most people would do. And I was determined not to raise and love my children the way I knew. Being comfortable being alone also means having the courage to stand up and be different. It means not being afraid to do the difficult thing.

Before my son was born, I reflected on the love I wanted as a child and never received, and I promised myself that I would always communicate that love to my children.

Although I've had struggles as a parent, and made my share of mistakes, it makes me proud to know that I've kept that promise. The love I've given my children has always been based on how I wanted to be loved, the love I knew would nurture them and lift them up.

Relationships with Men

Overcoming negative patterns also meant striving to keep my children's father in their lives. As I described in an earlier chapter, the men in my life have not always been trustworthy, or good role models for myself or my children.

When I think of the people in my life I turn to for strength and comfort, who I pour my heart out to in times of trouble, most are women. Whether it's a family member, one of many good friends I've made over the years, or even someone I'm connected with through business—a mentor or even my lawyer—most of my confidants are women.

It would be easy for me to conclude from that that all men are undependable, that men are no good. But when you become a parent, you have to think for someone more than yourself. What message would it send to my children—son *and* daughter—to act as if men will always let you down, that they can't be trusted, that only women can be depended upon?

That's why I feel so blessed that my children's father has always remained in their lives. For various reasons, we decided that staying together as a couple was not going to work out, but he is a good man and has remained in their lives as a father figure. I've never had to take him to court to force him to pay child support, as so many women have to do. He's given us so much more.

To this day he treats our daughter, who's now twenty-five, as if she were still a little girl, doting on her as if she were a ten-year-old. He's given her an example of what a father is. For my son, he can look and see an example of how a man who may have made mistakes, who can't offer the financial support he might like to, can nonetheless stand up and be present and be a great father to his children.

Already my children have had more love and support than I had growing up. I can't tell you how important that has been to me as they've grown and become responsible, conscientious young adults.

And every bit as important as their father's presence in their lives is their connection to his side of the family. They simply can't get a relationship to a grandfather from my side of the family. When they go over to their grandmother's house on their father's side they're welcomed in, seated at the dinner table. They all eat together and pray together. They've even gone on vacations together!

They've been blessed to have access to these kinds of role models and examples in their lives through both their father's side of the family and through their godmother, who has welcomed them in as if they were her very own children. On my side of the family, I simply can't offer these things. Just to have that extra source of love has been a blessing not only for them but for me: their growth and happiness and love are mine as well. So many men simply disappear, but their father didn't, and because he made the choice to be a part of their lives, they've received so much that they would not have otherwise.

At the same time, my own feelings and experiences with men who are absent and not reliable has been so unhealthy for me in my own life. I let myself internalize these sorts of messages about men. I still have these insecurities.

Learning from Mistakes

As I mentioned above, making mistakes as a parent is inevitable. What matters is how you respond to those mistakes.

One of the mistakes I sometimes feel I've made as a parent is to be too involved, too hands-on, in the lives of my children. The hardest thing for a parent to do is let go, to stand on the sidelines while their children fall.

As my children have become adults, I've become better at standing back and letting them have their own experiences, enjoying their triumphs and learning from their mistakes. At times I've had no choice but to stand off to the side and watch. But I think being a single parent, especially one who often had to spend time away creating a business that would support us all, made it particularly hard for me to keep out of my children's lives and let them rise and fall on their own power. I wanted so badly to give them every advantage, every opportunity, sometimes I lost sight of the need for them to discover things for themselves.

I know that my son, in particular, has sometimes felt that I've been controlling as a mother. We spoke about this recently and he thinks that the way I ran my business for many years made me want to manage the rest of my life in the same manner I ran my business.

I think he may be right. For a long time, I was extremely focused on managing every detail of my business, and the boundaries between my work life and home life were very thin—it's no surprise that I might have taken that same hands-on managing style and applied it to parenting as well.

As I've described in earlier chapters, until just recently, I handled every detail of my business. I was the go-to person for absolutely everything, responsible for every contract, every payment, in charge of making sure every box and computer and desk and office chair made it to the right place and on time. To say that I was detail-oriented would be an enormous understatement. At the same time, the nature of being so hands-on as an entrepreneur means that you can't leave work at work. Running your own business is not a nine-to-five job, and my business often came home with me. My family have memories of me responding to e-mails at midnight or answering a phone call at 2:30 in the morning.

Today, I've gotten much better at balancing my work and my life, but I can see how that might have come across to my children. When I wasn't sleeping, I was trying to anticipate, prevent, and solve problems at work, and to switch that part of me off when I came home just wasn't an option for a long time. If I came home from a day of fixing issues with a contract and solving problems on a job site and saw my son or daughter doing the wrong thing, missing opportunities, or just failing to live up to their God-given potential, I'm sure I didn't even consider standing on the sidelines and letting them fail. Letting them learn from their mistakes, or simply letting them know I loved them no matter what, might have been more helpful than trying to fix every problem or mistake I saw them struggling with.

Thankfully, as we've all grown older, I've gotten much better at trusting my children to do the right thing and make the right decision. I've watched them stumble and tried my best to let them trip and fall, knowing—and letting them know—that I'm standing by, ready and willing to help if they need it.

On the other end of the spectrum, a different sort of mistake or problem that's arisen from being a parent is withdrawing from the broader social life of my family, and shrinking the circle of friends in my life, because I was preoccupied with concern for my children.

I can't help what other people may think. Some people may have felt I was being distant or excluding them, but as many new parents have discovered, once you have children, your priorities change in an instant. I never set out to disrespect anyone, or let old friendships drift away, but at the same time, I would have done anything for my children. My own concerns and social life, the old obligations that used to be important to me, fell away in a second once I gave birth to my son.

But as I've learned many times in my life, mistakes and negative experiences only hold us back if we let them. If we're open to learning from every experience, good or bad, nothing can stop our growth. You hear so often today about women having to choose between having careers and having children. The implication is that one complicates the other, or that they're mutually exclusive.

For me it's been almost the exact opposite. Having children has given me focus and purpose. I might have started my business if I'd never had children, but I'm sure I wouldn't have had half the success I have had, because my *why* would not have been half as important to me.

I've been blessed to learn from my mistakes, and to let my children come to make their own. I've been blessed to watch them grow into the wonderful people they are today, finding their way in life.

Their caring for each other, their sensitivity to those around them, their love and compassion—all of this means that I have succeeded in the lessons I've tried to impart.

Every day, I pray to God to watch over each of them. For each is the greatest gift given to me in this world. Their lives are my blessing.

Chapter Ten

Raising Entrepreneurs

Everything in my life, good and bad, goes into the way I parent and love my children. For me to be there for my children, to connect with them and to teach them how to love and be loved, I can't hold back any part of myself. I just can't put up barriers between the different areas of my life.

That includes parenting and entrepreneurship, two of the great passions of my life. As my children become adults, it's become increasingly important for me to expose them to what it means to be an entrepreneur, both the good and the bad. One of the great satisfactions of being a parent, for me, is raising my children to value themselves and their ideas highly enough to bet on themselves, just as I did. Raising entrepreneurs is the focus of this chapter.

My friend commented before that I don't create walls between the different parts of my life. When things don't go right, he tells me, I really show it emotionally. If something big is going on at work—or in any other area of my life—the people around me are not only going to hear about it, we're going to sit down and talk about it and come up with a solution. As friends point out, it can be a good thing and a bad thing.

Bringing everything into my parenting and my home life can be a bad thing because sometimes you just want to come home and forget about what happened during the day, who said something foolish or unkind or who did you wrong. Striking the right balance between my work and the rest of my life has been a struggle for me, as I'll discuss in a future chapter. Sometimes you just want to leave work at work, and when doing that is a struggle, it can cause stress and complications.

But bringing everything home and talking about whatever is bothering me is a good thing, too, because it allows me to be true to myself. My children are not getting half a Tasha or a quarter of a Tasha. They're not getting a lot of small talk from me while my mind is a thousand miles away, worrying over something going on at work. That thing that's on my mind is always going to be what I talk about.

Being Realistic about Entrepreneurship

Sharing what's going on with me is also the best way I know to really give my children a sense of what it takes to run a business, manage people, find a market for what you do, and satisfy customers.

You might find books on entrepreneurship that will give you a rosy picture of starting your own business, selling this idea that it's easy. My children know better. That's because they've heard all the details from me, and they've seen up close how running a business the right way, doing things by the book and not cutting corners, can spill over a normal nine-to-five workday.

As I described in an earlier chapter, I'll be happy for my children if they decide that they don't want to make a career out of TBS. I'm happy to let them come and go, adjusting the hours they work for me to suit the needs of whatever other business ventures they have going on. If there's a big event or a big deadline coming up and they need to scale back their hours, no problem.

It gives me great satisfaction to know that I can let my children stand up and walk on their own, and if they happen to fall down trying out a new business venture, there's always a job at TBS for them to return to.

Believe it or not, I'd also be fine if my children decided they wanted to work a nine-to-five job in an office, reporting to a manager and collecting a monthly paycheck. I've seen the other side of the work world, starting my career in offices as a government employee. At the time, the security of having a job to return to was a great comfort, and a big improvement over working a retail job. From insurance and a retirement plan to having a set of work friends, there's nothing wrong with having a steady job.

(And believe me, from all the people who told me I was crazy to give up a steady government job, I have the list of benefits of these kinds of jobs memorized.)

Just so long as my children are happy in what they're doing, and they're working in a field or doing work that they feel passionate about, I have no problem with that decision.

In fact, I feel secure that if they decide to follow that route, they will do so having had a good exposure to the realities of entrepreneurship. I couldn't blame them if, having grown up listening to their mother's stories about unreliable subcontractors, clients who were late with payments, and any of a hundred other complications, they decided that the "normal" route worked better for them. That's especially true now that they've both become such integral parts of the business and have seen up close just what it takes to run a business.

The truth is, entrepreneurship simply isn't for everyone. Not everyone can cross over to the other side of the working world. I understand that.

With that said, I believe that both of my children have the inclination, the intelligence, the will, and the desire to be successful entrepreneurs and to nurture their own businesses into profitable ventures that bring them not only financial security but personal satisfaction and—just as important—give them a foundation from which to reach back and help others.

I've seen what they can do. I'm not just proud, I'm confident and impressed.

My children know what it takes to run a business. They've had front-row seats as TBS has grown from an idea into the thriving business it is today, and they've helped it to grow and flourish. As my children continue their own projects, and as they launch new ones in the future, they won't go forward with idealistic visions in their heads of easy riches and immediate success.

And again, that has a lot to do with me talking about what's on my mind. Even before they came on board with the company, my children knew all about some of the problem clients I have worked with in the past. They knew the special struggles I've faced as a black woman running a business in a field that's dominated by white men. I talked about everything with them, and when they began to help me, they saw it all firsthand.

That's the kind of exposure to entrepreneurship that many young people spend big money to obtain in business school.

Teaching by Example

At the same time that I've taught my children how to start businesses through my words, and through answering their questions about obtaining contracts or writing business plans, I believe the best lessons in entrepreneurship I've taught them have come through my example.

For most of their lives, they have seen their mother in control of everything from her own finances to how she spends her time. At this point, the days of worrying about a spiteful boss denying me a promotion, or a new congressional budget putting me out of work, are a distant memory.

My children have also spent most of their lives with a mother who is positive and happy about going to work in the morning, rather than slinking into the office full of dread over the day to come, or wishing it were still the weekend. Stepping forward and taking a positive, active role in creating your own future is at the heart of entrepreneurship.

Instead of worrying about what might or might not happen, entrepreneurs work to make whatever *does* happen the best that they can imagine. I believe and truly hope that that's something my children have seen and picked up on as they've lived and worked beside me.

With every moment and every choice, an entrepreneur has an influence on the way his or her life unfolds. Instead of being content to be a victim of circumstance, the entrepreneur finds ways to utilize each circumstance for meaningful, positive purposes. I may complain about this or that thing that happened at work during the day, but what do I go and *do* about it?

I'll talk more about mentorship in a future chapter, but the entrepreneur is also careful to seek out and choose who and what influences him or her. And even when we can't control every influence in our lives, we can absolutely control what we make of those various influences. I couldn't wish away the skin condition that put me in the hospital for all those painful surgeries, but what I have made of that experience was 100 percent within my control—and I wouldn't trade those lessons for anything in the world. As entrepreneurs we must make the choice, again and again, to make the best of our circumstances.

What I hope I have demonstrated to my children about entrepreneurship is that there is always a way forward—so take it! There is always something useful, valuable, and positive you can do—so do it, and get life going your way.

My Daughter the Entrepreneur

One thing my daughter has definitely inherited from me is that she does not enjoy working for other people for very long, unless it's a family business.

Cooking can be a thankless job, and to get anywhere you often have to put your time in, slowly moving up the ranks. It is a culture where you have to pay your dues. My daughter understands the nature of the business, and she has the patience and steady temperament to accept that she had to put in her time.

But she's no pushover, either, and she knows what she's worth. I was proud of her sense of strategy, but I was just as proud when she left that job after a few months, saying that she felt she was being taken advantage of by a management team that didn't appreciate her dedication and commitment. She is very passionate about her profession.

She told me she was over being "taken for granted," and I just had to smile. I know that feeling!

Right now she's helping me with TBS, but on the side she'll take up a kitchen job for a few months, dropping it and scaling back her hours at the business when her catering service suddenly picks up.

It's a clever way to build up her business, and I'm proud of her for being careful, slowly adding clients to her list and building an outstanding reputation through word of mouth. She saw her mother make a big leap into running her own business and she's doing it a little differently. My way isn't the only way, and I love that she's careful and methodical with her business so that she doesn't have to make the same kind of leap I did.

She was twelve when I started the business, old enough that she can clearly remember what things looked like before I decided to take my financial well-being into my own hands. She told me recently, "I want to be the boss, like my mom."

This Is Your Stepping-Stone

While the truth is that I hope my children will build long, successful careers as entrepreneurs, I understand that there are times that they might want to try something else. For my daughter, especially, her calling has occasionally taken her into accepting catering contracts and she's had to take a leave from TBS.

I always tell her the same thing: TBS will be here for you. This is your stepping-stone. As much as I value her contributions to the business, from having her as a sounding board to knowing I can go take care of something off-site because she's answering the phones or supervising a job, I value her happiness more. Looking at how entrepreneurship has changed and enriched my life, it's easy to encourage my children to pursue it themselves.

To be honest, if my son or daughter takes me aside and says, "I want to leave for a while and try X, Y, or Z," that can be an uncomfortable conversation. I'm happy for them, don't get me wrong, and I support them. But as a mother I'm prone to worrying and second-guessing, and as an experienced businesswoman I might have some serious doubts—I might feel like I can see complications and problems they just can't see. (Not to mention how much I value their contributions to TBS!)

But one way I've grown and matured over the years of trying to help them in their own careers is learning to accept that I've got to let them go out and try different things. They may fail. They may come back to the nest with ruffled feathers or a broken wing. That's what I'm here for, and I'm so glad to be able to offer them that landing pad. Without it, how much more difficult and daunting it would be to ever try to get their own businesses off the ground. To offer your children opportunities you never had is the dream of every parent, and I feel so blessed to be able to do just that by giving them a job they can always return to.

I've even applied this philosophy to some of my employees, telling them that TBS is their stepping-stone, and if they want to leave and try something else, *great*. TBS will always be here if it doesn't work out. I might miss the good work that those employees performed, but nothing can match the feeling of knowing that I helped them get to a position of spreading their wings to fly away.

My Son the Entrepreneur

As I've written about my son and his journey to becoming the entrepreneur he is today, I can't take too much credit for him launching his line of clothing and custom apparel.

God deserves much of the credit—my son needed to stop what he was doing and sit and talk with God. The results speak for themselves.

But my son also deserves recognition for being open to what God had to say, and to being willing to examine his life, think about the path he was on, and change his direction before he went even further down the road he'd been traveling.

Some of that experience is expressed in the clothing that my son's company produces. It's all about turning your dreams into reality, he explained to me when he debuted his clothing designs. It's based on his experience, growing from being a mover for TBS to running his own business. Whatever you want in life, you can do it if you're motivated enough.

That wasn't always his outlook on life. Before his incarceration, my son simply wasn't the self-starter he is today. I've described the way he approached his work with TBS during those first big jobs. He was a hard worker, thorough and trustworthy, but as far as showing the initiative and interest to advance to the next level, to be someone who wants to know all the details and read over the fine print of contracts and be a manager with the power to hire and fire people—he just wasn't there yet.

When he came back, though, he was a changed man. The experience he went through woke him up and gave him the ability to get up on his feet and truly *want* to do something.

Does that sound familiar? I don't know how many times, navigating the world of government and small businesses, I've seen other entrepreneurs who have the capital, the business-school education, even the right clothes and business jargon fail because they lack the desire. Simple as it may sound, they just don't want to succeed badly enough to do all the little things to take them there. *Wanting it* is at the heart of my story, and now it's at the heart of my son's.

I can't tell you how relieved I was to talk to my son after his return and discover how much he wanted and even needed to build something of his own. It made me so proud and so grateful to be able to offer my son a job as soon as he got out. Young men who have been to prison face truly daunting obstacles in finding jobs and transitioning back into society—the nonprofit organization I founded, the Phoenix Reintegration Project, is dedicated to addressing this very problem, as I'll discuss in a later chapter—and I was so very pleased to be able to offer my son gainful employment from the moment he came home.

But even though my son could still have a fine career, helping me to run TBS and perhaps even running it after I retire, what I want for him, as well as my daughter, is for him to identify what he's passionate about and to build a business—perhaps several businesses—from that.

That's at the heart of why I want to raise entrepreneurs. But it's also just the foundation for what entrepreneurship can give them. Of course I want them to build financial security for themselves. But I also want them to have the freedom and flexibility to run their businesses as they see fit, looking out for the right opportunities and creating opportunities for themselves, rather than simply waiting for whatever comes along.

Most importantly, I want them to use their businesses to help others. To reach out into the community and pull up men and women who could use a job, who have been overlooked or unfairly discriminated against, who are trying hard and have families to feed.

As I often tell my children, I'm raising *employers*, not *employees*.

When I look at my son's example, I also see my own story in the way that adversity has strengthened him. Just as I became stronger from spending so many summer days alone indoors, by being overlooked and forgotten, feeling ugly and unloved, and from experiencing such sheer physical pain, I believe my son's experience has galvanized the strength and potential that were already in him and given him the ability to channel his power into the right outlets, to do things the right way.

Since he returned and joined me at TBS, my son has become an invaluable part of the business's day-to-day operations. In a previous chapter, I contrasted him to my nephew, who wanted to learn everything about the computer systems that we were disconnecting and moving from one place to another; over time, my nephew learned all there was to know about these systems, and today he's an accomplished IT professional.

What I see now is that my son simply wasn't in the right place to do the same thing as my nephew. With time and guidance, however, he's there now, engaged in every facet of the business, gifted with mature judgment and a sharp-eyed understanding of the details of what we do at TBS.

His intelligence, steady leadership, and understanding are a constant gift to me. Because he's my son, it gives me pride and pleasure to see him thriving. As the business's owner, every detail that I can pass off to him, or to my daughter, without having to worry and check in every twenty minutes, frees up that much more time and energy for me to pursue new opportunities, think about ways to expand and improve the business, or simply take a little time for myself.

At the same time that talking to God drove my son's maturation process, he is such a good, humble young man that he's quick to point to the effect that my example had on him. I gave him the inspiration to get in his own lane, he tells me, and start his own business. Based on what I've done and what I've been through, he knows he has the strength, knowledge, and experience to build a successful business of his own.

He knows I'm there to help, that if I can do anything for him and his business, from answering questions to looking over contracts, I'll do it without hesitation. It can be difficult not to want to hold his hand or give him advice, but seeing him doing such a fine job at TBS brings me peace as far as knowing that he can make his own business decisions.

The Long Haul

There are two lessons about entrepreneurship that too often get overlooked when people talk about running a business, and that I hope and believe my children are in a unique position to learn from me.

The first is that overnight successes are made through years and years of hard work. I was very fortunate, early in my career, to land a number of big contracts, jobs that not only brought in substantial payments to TBS but gave my business a platform and—when we'd done a phenomenal job—to earn meaningful praise from very important and influential people. But for each of those "lucky breaks" I put in hours and hours of time marketing my business, researching companies and government regulations, and in general putting myself in a position to act quickly when the time was right.

At the same time, for many years, TBS was essentially a one-woman operation. As I described before, it's only been very recently that I've been able to bring my children on board. For the first decade of running TBS, I did virtually everything. Today, TBS brings in more than $1.5 million in annual revenue, but it certainly didn't happen overnight. And there was never any guarantee that it would happen, not without me worrying over every detail, taking every call, answering every e-mail, sometimes working all night to make sure everything was in order prior to a big job.

I truly hope my children have learned these lessons from me. These kinds of insights are easy to *tell* young entrepreneurs, and easy to hear, but so much more difficult to internalize or to truly accept. Many people who start businesses see the glamorous aspects of being their own boss, focusing on the flexibility to work whenever they want, wherever they want. And of course they see the money that comes with running things.

They're overlooking not only the hard work they'll need to put in, but how long they might have to put in that work before they can even approach the level of success, satisfaction, and material comfort they have in mind.

From having watched their mother put in the hard work, day in and day out, over the better part of a decade, I sincerely hope my children will understand the resilience they'll need to show to keep on the right path, to keep pushing forward with their own businesses. I hope that my example will inspire them to know not merely that it can be done, but that they have the strength and inner resources to be the ones to do it.

The second lesson about entrepreneurship is one I've mentioned before, and that is *giving back*.

This is a lesson I feel confident both my son and my daughter have learned from the time they were little. Even before I started my own business, giving back to the community and helping others in one way or another has been important to me and to my family. As I've built a bigger platform to help the people around me, the only thing that's changed has been the scale of giving back and the amount of good we're able to do.

Entrepreneurship is about so much more than money, as I've already mentioned. It's no wonder you hear people talking about *cultural entrepreneurship* and *social entrepreneurship*: these ideas of raising the capital to help others, build awareness, and empower the people around you are incredibly potent, and I hope any young entrepreneur—whether it's my children or a stranger reading this—will think hard about how to use this potential to its fullest effect.

To be honest, I already see my children incorporating these ideas into their entrepreneurial pursuits. My daughter's catering business is a brilliant way of engaging with families and couples, cooking for them on an intimate scale and facilitating meaningful social occasions that they'll remember for years to come. And my son's clothing line is built around spreading a message of positivity and working hard to achieve your dreams.

For so many parents, there can be an attitude of "Do what I say, not what I do," reflecting the fact that we don't want our children to copy us.

I feel so blessed to look at the lives my children have built and see the best parts of my life and myself reflected there. I am proud to think that, with me as their example, they are doing well *and* doing good in their careers.

Chapter Eleven

The Phoenix Reintegration Project

In another chapter, I mentioned all the young men I refer to as my nephews: young men who come through my house, who work for me, who call me "Aunt Tay" when they see me out and about.

Although I only have one nephew who is an actual blood relation, calling these young men my nephews is closer to the truth than most might think. I care for these young men. Their hardships are mine, and so are their triumphs. I know their struggles and I see the good in them.

With some of these nephews, I see the good through the labels that society has put on them. Unemployable. Ex-convict. Felon. Criminal.

For most of the time it has been in business, TBS has made it a point to hire young men who have recently returned from prison.

After reading the last chapter and my description of my son's experience, you'll understand why treating returned young men with respect is important to me, and why I feel confident that these young men deserve a second chance.

More broadly than that, though, hiring these young men has always been a key way to do just what I've talked about in prior chapters: reaching back and helping others. Trying to be a force for good in my community.

As I've gotten more comfortable using my platform as a business owner to do more than just earn money, though, I've started to see the limitations of helping these young men simply through hiring them.

Hiring these men gives them a chance to feed their families, and in some cases it sets them on the path to a solid new career. But what about those I'm not able to hire? Are there others in the community I'm leaving out? How can I help the families of these men who have been sent to prison?

Recognizing these gaps is what led me to found my nonprofit organization, the Phoenix Reintegration Project (PRP).

The PRP's mission is to help returning citizens transition back into the workforce—and the community. Through PRP we provide training that helps individuals build confidence and opens up job prospects, paving the way toward economic empowerment.

PRP is truly my passion project. I spoke in another chapter about finding my *why*—PRP and the work we do for these returning citizens is truly at the heart of my *why*.

Why This Cause Is Close to My Heart

My son is truly blessed.

I know a lot of people might not agree that anyone who spent three years in prison could be lucky, but I know it's true. In the last chapter I described God sitting down and having a talk with him, and the changed man who emerged when he was released. Not everyone is capable of having that conversation—of really listening and changing. Of growing up.

But my son was also blessed that he always had a job waiting for him once he left prison. That might not sound like a big deal, but anyone who knows the trials that await returned citizens will know it's a *very* big deal.

The hoops and obstacles that await a young man just out of prison are enough to make your head spin. In most states, you're required to get a job within your first thirty days. To apply for most jobs, you'll need some form of identification. But if you are someone who doesn't have the benefit of a supportive family, ready to give you a place to live even though you have no money, it's going to be tough to get that ID without a place to live. And until you can get a job and earn some money, you're going to struggle to put a roof over your head.

There are other complications as well. Many of the young men coming out of prison are illiterate, or at the very least unfamiliar with using the computer—which is the one and only way many workplaces want you to apply for work. There are resources out there to help people in these positions, but again, if you're someone without a strong support network, unable to read, there's a strong chance you'll never know of those resources.

And all of this is ignoring the "elephant in the room": many employers simply don't want to hire young men who have been to prison. Job applicants are required to disclose that they have been to prison. In a competitive job market, it's inevitable that a hiring manager looking at two very similar resumes, trying to decide between two equally qualified applicants, is going to want to avoid taking a risk on the applicant who's just returned from prison.

These are all the reasons I say that my son was lucky. He was able to report to his probation officer immediately that he had a job, he had somewhere to stay.

From my work through Phoenix, and from having known many returned citizens growing up, I know that many of these young men come home with the best of intentions only to grow frustrated at the obstacles that stand in their way. I truly can't blame them.

If I had the opportunity and the resources to make it easier on these young men, and give them a foothold as they try to pick themselves up, just like my son had, how could I refuse to try?

How TBS Supports Returned Citizens

As I said, my son's experience made me want to help others. But I met my husband while he was on house arrest, and after he went to federal prison I had a job waiting for him upon his release. As with my son, I knew his heart and I knew him to be a good man. It was a blessing to be able to support them both and give them each a start on a new life.

Having them in my mind helps me to see through those labels that society puts on these men. If I need movers for a big job, I will talk to one of these young men and judge whether I think he will be a good, hard worker based on the answers he gives me and my feel for him. If I have a good feeling about a job applicant, I'm not going to get scared off by what's in his past.

Nowadays, as I've said, I entrust a lot of the business's day-to-day operations to my children. My son, in particular, makes a lot of decisions about who to hire (and even, sometimes, who to fire).

He's proven his judgment to me many times over, and he knows better than anyone my attitude about hiring returned citizens. If an applicant passes my son's test, he's hired.

By the same token, I hold these employees to the same standard I hold anyone else I hire. You're here to do a job. That's what I'm paying you for. Do your job and do it well and we'll get along beautifully. If not, well—as I mentioned in an earlier chapter, my philosophy is "I don't fire anyone. *You* fire you."

At the end of the day, TBS is a business. It's wonderful to use this platform I have built to lift up the people around me, but if I start letting subpar work slide because I like the person, that's when your platform starts to sink.

Doing More Good

The seeds for the Phoenix Reintegration Project were planted on the day that the judge handed down my son's sentence. Close to thirty family members and friends from the church and the community were there with me at the courthouse, supporting my family and me. As crushed as I was, hearing that sentence read out, even in such a low moment, I knew that something good could come of this.

At that exact moment, I couldn't know what shape that good outcome would take. It took my son returning home, and seeing the kind of support he enjoyed that so many others don't, for the gears to start turning in my mind.

While I was always happy to hire returned citizens for TBS jobs, it wasn't a company policy. It wasn't something that I did actively.

As the business has grown, it's been a blessing to help more and more returning men by giving them jobs and training. But there's a limit to how many people I can help.

The more good I did, the more I yearned to do good on a larger scale, to help even more of these young men to get back on their feet, to make something of themselves, to reintegrate into society.

I began looking for ways to help even when I didn't have jobs to offer. I said, "How can I help even if I can't give these men a way to put food on the table?" And I thought, "If I can't hire them, I can at least train them."

This is how the Phoenix Reintegration Project was born. Through TBS, and from my own money, I was able to provide the financial support to fund and run PRP and we began offering a number of valuable accreditations for returning citizens.

At PRP part of our mission is to financially support each member and provide the training and accreditation needed to find jobs such as management specialists, support service administrators, and general supply contractors.

As that old saying goes, give a man a fish and he'll eat for a day—but if you teach a man to fish, he'll eat for a lifetime. Some of the best employees I've ever had have been returned citizens, and they've told me many times how grateful they are that I gave them a chance to show what they could do, to prove who they really were, at a time when not many employers were willing to do so.

But winning employees' loyalty is the furthest thing from my mind when I reach out to these young men. I'd like to think that even if a returned citizen never works a minute for TBS, adding that certification to his resume might just help make the difference between a hiring manager throwing his application away and calling him in for an interview.

As I said in a prior chapter, I hope TBS and the Phoenix Reintegration Project can be these returnees' stepping-stone. If a man can get training, work for me to feed his family, and a month or a year down the road that training, that resume experience, lets him get a high-paying job operating a forklift in a warehouse? I wish him luck! (And if he never works for me, I wish him luck just the same!)

The Philosophy Behind PRP

My approach to founding the Phoenix Reintegration Project was gradual, a natural outgrowth of what I saw around me.

But the organization is helping to address a much bigger problem, one that everyone from prison administrators to researchers and congressmen have been grappling with for some time.

A key job of prison administrators is to offer programming that will support offenders as they return to the community. Policymakers also want to decrease recidivism, especially as prisons fill at an alarming rate and the funding for building and operating new facilities grows more and more scarce.

As a result, more attention is being paid to resources that will help offenders reenter their communities successfully. Programs and interventions that increase "self-efficacy"—the belief that you can succeed in a given situation—can dramatically improve a returning citizen's odds of succeeding at reintegrating into the community. That's where PRP comes in.

Unfortunately, building up a returning citizen's sense of self-efficacy isn't easy. Prison imposes a strict daily schedule on an inmate, so that upon leaving that environment it can be easy to be overwhelmed by the choices facing them. And after a few months or years in prison, the returning citizen may find that the support networks he had in place before are no longer there. He's starting from nothing, with little to no support and a lot of pressure to succeed.

A program like the Phoenix Reintegration Project fills a critical crack in the system, one that a lot of young men just out of prison fall into. The Project offers returning citizens a pathway to restoring their sense of self-respect and self-worth, increasing their chances of becoming productive, contributing members of society and decreasing the odds of returning to a life of crime. We're working to disrupt that cycle of crime and imprisonment.

The unfortunate fact is that this issue affects my community and my family directly. It's not abstract, the way it is for a lot of researchers and policymakers. Statistically, African Americans are incarcerated at a far higher rate than other racial groups—more than five times the rate at which whites are incarcerated, according to the National Association for the Advancement of Colored People (NAACP). And a criminal record can reduce the chances of a callback for a job interview by as much as 50 percent, and those rates are even higher for African Americans (also per the NAACP).

It would be easy to feel powerless, reading statistics like those, or to get angry.

But I can't accept those responses. Not if that's all you do. Not if it keeps you from doing something real to help the people around you.

I refuse to demonize these people I grew up with, these people I love.

I believe in second and third chances, and I see the good in people. Too often, for returning citizens, that second chance is no real chance at all, and they come out of prison to find the deck stacked against them.

Giving them a chance, building them up so they can feel good about themselves and their ability to support themselves and the people they love, that's at the heart of the Phoenix Reintegration Project's mission.

Successes

I'm so proud of all the good we've done through the PRP.

We've had men who went through PRP-supported training who today own their own businesses. Others have gone back to school and earned degrees. One young man—I count him as one of my "nephews"—left TBS to start his own nonprofit organization, helping others. At least one other young man went on to become a pastor.

These stories, to me, define success for an endeavor like the PRP.

As this initiative has grown and evolved, we've also been able to do a lot of good through a number of different campaigns that have expanded our mission to helping the community in general.

We started with an annual Thanksgiving campaign that has become a tradition. Collecting donations of food and money, we provide Thanksgiving Baskets to families in the community who may struggle to provide a traditional Thanksgiving meal to their children. Each basket contains a turkey and all the ingredients needed to provide a memorable meal for a family of six, along with a roasting pan to do it in. The Department of Social Services gives us the names and addresses of families in need in our community. And we enlist lots of people in distributing the baskets, making it an inclusive event that involves the whole community.

Since that first Thanksgiving food drive we've added more campaigns to help the community: just recently we held a winter coat drive and also collected hats, gloves, scarves, and other

148 | Finding My Why

cold-weather essentials, which we handed out on the streets of Washington, D.C., Maryland, and Virginia.

We also held a very successful campaign called Soles4Souls that collected donations of shoes. The campaign was inspired by the advice that you can't really judge someone until you've walked a mile in his shoes, and we were able to collect shoes, as well as shirts and T-shirts, to donate to a small village in Ghana. The event helped us to get the word out about the Phoenix Reintegration Project's mission.

And this past summer, we threw our first annual block party, which we saw as a day of unity for Prince George's County residents. The event featured food, shopping, and performances by local DJs and musicians. The block party was a tremendous success, bringing out residents of all ages and raising awareness of the Phoenix Reintegration Project—as well as $5,000 to use to pay for a returning citizen to attend Commercial Driver's License (CDL) school.

What the Future Holds

As the PRP builds a reputation for helping young men get back on their feet, and as more people in the community come into contact with us and the valuable work we do, I have high hopes that we can continue to make a difference.

Every dollar that we raise through our various campaigns, as well as private donations, we pour back into the PRP's work. TBS also supports the PRP financially. I'm extremely excited about the future of the Phoenix Reintegration Project and the good work we can continue to do.

From the beginning, my philosophy toward TBS and the PRP has been that I want to do all the good I possibly can. TBS wins the contracts and PRP trains the community to be able to work as employees on those contracts. It's truly a win-win situation.

I want to help as many people and touch the lives of as many folks in my community as I am able to do. There's no quota or goal for the nonprofit organization. It's simply about doing good while I have the chance, and the means, to do so.

I do this for my community. I do it for all my "nephews," even the nephews I haven't met yet.

But the good this work does me is immeasurable. It soothes my soul to do this work.

Entrepreneurship has never been about the money for me. It's about what it allows me to do:

Set my own course. Hire who I want to hire. Support the society in which I live. And help everyone I possibly can.

When challenges occur, what drives me forward is not increasing revenue for my business, or pumping up my personal bank account. It's figuring out how to provide value to my family and the community where I live and work. It's helping one more person that could really use it. That's what pushes me to overcome each challenge.

Chapter Twelve

Teaching Young People to Be Entrepreneurs

The first chapters of this book revolved around the negative words that I once allowed to define me. *Forgotten. Ugly. Pain. Lonely.* And so many more that reflect the struggles of my childhood.

Beginning when I first left home, and continuing as I got a job of my own, raised a family, and started my own business, I've come to define myself and my life more positively. Who can I help with the gifts I have been given? What good can I do with my platform? How can I view the situation around me and find the potential for good in it? These are the thoughts, the questions that guide me in my present life. Today, it's all about the potential to do good, help others, save souls.

But I haven't forgotten those early years, including the negatives. Whether it's drawing the strength to stand alone, firm in my convictions, from all the days when I was left truly alone, or recognizing the love I want my children and myself to experience based on the love I longed for when I was younger, I continue to draw strength from *all* my experiences, good and bad.

That's a major part of what drives me to teach others entrepreneurship and the fundamentals of business. Whether it's young people in my community, family members, TBS employees, or returning citizens who find me through my work with the Phoenix Reintegration Project, part of what drives me to help them is the vivid memory of just what it was like to be in their position.

I still remember just how little I knew about business when I started TBS. Looking on the internet for business plans and contracts that I could use. The mistakes I made, just trying to figure things out. The sleepless nights before those first, important jobs, and the nervous energy in the pit of my stomach when we started those jobs.

I don't look back on those early days so I can pat myself on the back and congratulate myself on everything I've accomplished. That gives me a good feeling, but reflecting on past triumphs, reliving those good feelings, is not what drives an individual or a business forward.

What stirs up my passion to teach others to be entrepreneurs is realizing I have a unique opportunity: I can still remember how it felt to just be getting started, to have so many questions, to not know who to turn to. At the same time, I know the answers now, and I'm happy to share them.

More than that, I feel it's my duty to share those answers. As I said in a previous chapter, I'm in the business of saving souls.

Teaching others what I know is just one fantastic way God has given me of doing that.

The Power of Mentoring

When I mention feeling that I didn't get a whole lot of support from my family and the people around me, I'm not trying to embarrass anyone or settle scores. In a lot of cases, the people in my community and in my home didn't know how to write a business plan, set up a limited liability corporation, or attain a certain status with the federal government. There simply were not a lot of people around me growing up who ran their own businesses. As the saying goes, *You don't know what you don't know.*

That same idea extends to how people responded when they heard I was going to quit my steady, dependable job with the federal government to start my own business. They asked me if I was crazy, pled with me not to do this, and warned me that I'd be living on someone's couch in a matter of months.

Naturally, it makes me happy that I proved them all wrong. But the reason that I mention this again is that these kinds of predictions, this lack of support, goes hand in hand with a lack of experience. To the outside, to people who didn't know the first thing about what it takes to run a business, what I was about to do *did* look crazy.

That's because you can't imagine being what you never see around you. The people in my life had hardly ever seen anyone quit their job and start their own successful business, so of course what I did looked to them like someone going crazy and quitting a good job.

This is exactly why mentorships are so important. You can read about how to start a business, and you can find other people's business plans on the internet. But without a real, flesh-and-blood person to look to as a model, or to ask questions, or to run ideas past, you're going to end up a little lost, and more than likely you will make mistakes that you could otherwise have avoided. If you're lucky, your business will survive those mistakes long enough for you to learn from them. If you're not, well, you may simply be out of luck.

The Importance of Mentoring in My Career

In an earlier chapter, I described the importance of working with Ms. Shirley Blair, the founder of Blair Temporaries and Staffing, Inc., and the founder of Minorities in the Temporary Industry, a consortium of women and minority staffing companies, at a crucial juncture in my business. At that time, I had only recently founded my business. You could say that I was beginning to understand everything I didn't know about running a company.

That's exactly why I feel so blessed to have worked with Ms. Blair. She had an impressive track record not only of running her own business, but of building strong and meaningful support for others, in her own industry and well beyond it. She had an equally impressive record of turning around and helping other businesses owned by women and people of color. She made it her mission to take five companies per year and essentially take them under her wing, helping those business owners get from wherever they were to the place they wanted to be.

One of the first lessons I learned from Shirley Blair was that there wasn't any "right" or "wrong" goal to shoot for when it came to my business. For some entrepreneurs, their goal was getting from zero dollars in sales to $1 million. For someone else, the goal might be going from $1 million to $10 million. For still others, the goal might not be to keep growing revenues but to improve efficiency so that they could have more free time, or give back to the community. Ms. Blair helped me expand my vision, showing me that it wasn't just about growing more and more each year. It wasn't just about money.

I've always tried to give back, but working with Ms. Blair planted a seed in me. It was this idea that the goals of my business could be whatever I wanted them to be that started me along the path toward viewing TBS not just as a source of financial security, not just as a secure job, but a platform from which I could do good and serve others.

And her example, turning around and taking young entrepreneurs under her wing and sharing with them all she knew, inspired me to set higher goals for myself. Once I'm able to help others, I vowed, that's exactly what I'm going to do.

Ms. Blair took me with her on a number of trips to meet different people at different companies and agencies. My outlook was that I wanted to be a sponge and soak up as many of these experiences as I possibly could, retain as much of what she was teaching me, and make as many meaningful contacts as I could. Much of TBS's success, I would say, is based on how well I accomplished those goals during my time of being mentored by Ms. Blair.

Overall, it was an eye-opening experience, one that exposed me to many of the pitfalls and difficulties of running your own business. But seeing this unvarnished side of entrepreneurship, a "warts and all" look at founding and growing your own business, ultimately helped me in developing realistic expectations and knowing exactly what I was up against as I set to work building TBS.

Here's a good example of the kind of "real world" lessons I gained from working with a mentor. One of the key lessons Ms. Blair instilled in me was that as an entrepreneur, you cannot be afraid, or easily intimidated, when working with clients or prospective clients. Now, I was not so new to running my own business that I was afraid of conflict, but Ms. Blair helped me to put the matter into perspective. So many starting entrepreneurs walk on eggshells around prospective clients, afraid to say or do anything to upset these companies, agencies, and individuals whose business they are hoping to win. What Ms. Blair showed me was that that is a limiting perspective that puts the entrepreneur forever on the defensive, bending over backwards in an effort not to offend any potential client.

After working with Ms. Blair, I developed an attitude of "I don't need you to give me any business, just get out of my way." It's an attitude that has stuck with me through the years.

That's because working with her opened my eyes to just how many business opportunities there really are out there. As a new entrepreneur, it can be natural to think that every meeting with a potential client is "do or die," that if you don't get this contract you'll soon go bankrupt. What I learned from paying attention to what my mentor showed me was that if you network, keep your eyes open, and do good work, there are enough opportunities that you don't have to work with clients who intimidate you, lowball you on your fees, or treat you with disrespect. You can have the confidence to say *Just get out of my way.*

Just as beneficial as the new perspectives I gained from working with Ms. Blair was the affirmation she gave me, basically reinforcing the practices and characteristics that had led me to found my own business in the first place.

She applauded what she called my "stick-to-it-iveness." I have always taken the approach that if I take on a task, I'm going to see it through. Hearing from a seasoned professional what a valuable trait this is gave me a powerful feeling of encouragement.

Ms. Blair also saw that I had a strong grasp of the core of my business, but if I saw other opportunities that lay outside that core area, I was smart and brave enough to say, "I haven't done that yet, but I can learn." So many of those first, important jobs came from that positive attitude and the willingness to commit to doing my homework so that, even if TBS had never done this particular kind of job before, we could show up on the day of the move with the knowledge, competence, and confidence to leave the client completely satisfied.

How I Mentor Others

I've tried to apply the lessons from working with Shirley Blair to my own exchanges and hands-on work with young entrepreneurs.

What did she do that made me feel smart, capable, and confident? What lessons have stuck with me years later? What did she show me that I could never have read in a book, that I never would have figured out on my own? These are the kinds of lessons I want to impart when I work with young entrepreneurs as a mentor.

Just as important, though, is thinking back to before Ms. Blair mentored me, remembering what it was like when I didn't yet know all that I know now. I try to remain connected to those first days in business and use those memories and sensations to help me better connect with the young entrepreneurs who seek me out for advice.

All along my journey, when I've been able to help others with their businesses, I have done so without reservation. Whether it's looking over a business plan, listening as someone explains their business, conducting a mock interview, or meeting so that a young would-be entrepreneur can ask me questions about the entrepreneurship process, I've always been happy to do it. Recently

I've added public speaking and Facebook Live sessions to my busy schedule in hopes that I might inspire a young entrepreneur, or reach someone out there who has questions but doesn't quite know where to begin.

I've also been sure to end all of those conversations with the offer to stay in touch, and for these aspiring business owners to call me with questions, to let me know if I can help. When I worked with Shirley Blair, she made the same offer to help if I ever found that clients weren't paying, I was having trouble with employees, or any other problem that sprang up. With her experience, she'd seen just about everything and could talk me through every little snag or problem that could possibly occur. I don't doubt that if I were to call her up today with a problem, she'd be eager to help. That's true mentorship, and it's been important to me to offer the same help to the people I mentor—and to follow through on those promises.

In many cases, I've heard back from these people months and even years later, not just with questions or requests for help, but with success stories.

Just recently, I heard from a young entrepreneur who wanted to thank me for helping him. He wrote, "I greatly appreciate you for giving me the opportunity to learn. I was in one of the worst times of my life . . . I'm forever grateful to you."

What people may not realize is that receiving thanks, hearing from someone that your words and actions have been beneficial, is an immense reward to the mentor. That saying, heard usually around Christmastime, that it is better to give than to receive, is true the rest of the year as well. For me that's partly true because helping others puts me back in that mental state I had when I first started out, and gives me the feeling of relief and excitement that I had when Shirley Blair began to help me.

As I said, I've always made myself available on an informal basis to help young entrepreneurs. Over the last several years, though, as I've been able to look at the bigger picture of my business and my life and as I have actively sought out ways to make a more lasting impression on the lives of the people around me, I've made my mentoring activities more formal and official.

In 2015 I began the first Returning Citizens Entrepreneur Camp. The Camp is a free four-week program that educates returning citizens on the role of entrepreneurship, what it means to found and run your own business, and what skills and attributes are required to successfully found a business of your own.

Our goal with the Camp is to prepare returned citizens not to depend on employers but to create opportunities to control their own financial well-being and, ultimately, attain a position to help others. As I've described in previous chapters, not only my own story but that of my son have inspired me to reach out to these men in the hopes of helping them build up the confidence to forge their own paths.

While there is only so much anyone can learn about entrepreneurship during a four-week camp, what we offer is thorough and gives these men a strong foundation in all aspects of business. I find it especially important to cover these topics not in an abstract or overly academic fashion, but to focus on what these men really need to know: what do they have to do to incorporate their businesses and protect themselves from liability? What kinds of paperwork do they have to fill out, and what kinds of tax deadlines should they be aware of?

Again, my approach to this form of mentoring is driven by all that I didn't know when I started out. Marketing, networking, and the ins and outs of the tax code are among a number of topics that I found daunting as a new business owner. It gives me a great feeling of satisfaction to walk the students through these subjects, and many more.

Just as important, through the camp I build relationships with each of these returning citizens that are sustained and nurtured over time. Some of these men may go on to work for TBS—as I said, I'm happy to be someone's stepping-stone—while others jump right into businesses of their own. Wherever their paths lead, I make sure that graduates of the camp know that they can reach out anytime for whatever help I can give them.

The Importance of Taking Action

One thing I stress in my work with the Returning Citizens Entrepreneurship Camp is that all the advice and tips they're about to hear mean nothing without taking action. I give the same advice to the young people who reach out to me individually for advice, and it's exactly what I have tried to get across to my children: you can have an expensive business-school education but without taking that leap of faith, without putting yourself out there and offering your goods or service to the public, you're destined to fail.

It sounds so obvious, you would think no one would ever make such a simple mistake. But I see this all the time: people who know all the latest theories and case studies about business, finance, marketing, etc., backwards and forwards, but who are petrified to make a move. They're so afraid to fail, to lose money, that they freeze up.

Or to put it more bluntly, as I recently wrote to my friends on Facebook: "There are people less qualified than you doing things that you want to do, and the only difference between you and them is that they took ACTION and decided to believe in themselves. PERIOD. Stop talking and start doing."

Now, don't get me wrong. If you don't know the first thing about business, and you just put yourself out there and start a business without giving it a moment's thought, you're probably headed toward failure. Action and planning is not an either/or proposition. You need both to succeed.

But if I had to invest in a person with a lot of passion and the willingness to make something happen, and someone without those qualities, I know where I'd put my money.

Other words of wisdom I like to share:

We exist rather than thrive and we leave this world with a whimper instead of a bang!

Few of us explore our potential.

We all live lives of infinite potential but few of us make the most of our talent and resources.

Explore, plan, and react (react: "To act in opposition to a former condition or act").

Imagine what you could achieve if only you had the opportunity?

You do—but you have to explore, plan, and react.

How different could your life be if you would just explore, plan, and react?

Nobody should hold you back from reaching your potential.

So what is it that's holding you back? Maybe you need to understand yourself a little better?

Perhaps it's a friend or a relation, a husband or wife?

Or maybe, just maybe, it's YOU?

Isn't it time you found out and did something about it?

I'm very grateful for what I have been blessed with thus far. I will continue to aspire to be more. I will continue to sow seeds and "pay forward." This fire will continue to burn.

Life is for living and doing it on your own terms.

We all deserve to be happy and happiness comes from being fulfilled and doing the things that have meaning to us.

Remember, Do Life! Don't let Life Do you.

Or, as I also wrote to my friends recently:

"Good morning. There are those that make things happen, those that watch things happen, and those that don't know what's happening."

I know which of those groups I belong in, and my goal when others trust me enough to be their mentor is to help them get into the proper group as well.

Chapter Thirteen

Work-Life Balance

If you had asked me five years ago how I balanced my business with my personal life, I would have laughed.

If you'd asked me ten years ago, I wouldn't have even understood the question.

"But my business *is* my life," I probably would have said.

It makes a lot of sense that one of the last chapters in this book should be about maintaining work-life balance. It's really only been in the last few years that I've even noticed an imbalance in my life, much less set about correcting it.

Regardless, it's an important topic, especially for entrepreneurs and especially for female entrepreneurs, like myself, for whom family is their highest priority.

It's no mystery why entrepreneurs often have a poor work-life balance. When you're responsible for every detail of your own livelihood, work just naturally takes over the rest of your life.

That's how it's been for me. Over the twelve years that I've been building and growing TBS, it's become inevitable for me to think about business twenty-four hours a day, seven days a week. As I've said elsewhere in this book, for much of the time that I've been a business owner, every job was my responsibility.

Not only that, but TBS has always grown on the basis of our reputation. *My* reputation. If we aren't exceeding expectations, finding ways not just to move the client's offices seamlessly from one location to another but to set them up for success, we're going to fall to the middle of the pack.

That means every detail has got to be accounted for, every contract has to be checked and checked again, and every member of the team has to know exactly what he or she is doing once the job begins. Neither the work nor the responsibility can be passed to anyone else. As the saying goes, *The buck stops here.*

Does all that sound like something I can just leave at the office at 5 p.m.?

Being in charge of a business that depends so heavily on logistics is a recipe for stress. For many years, the only antidote to that stress was to work harder, put in more hours, to make sure that everything went smoothly and the customer wasn't just satisfied, but eager to tell everyone what an excellent job we'd done.

Over the course of this chapter, I'll describe some of the negative effects of having a work-life balance that's not actually balanced at all. And I'll talk about how I came to put my life into better balance with my work.

Why Balance Is So Important

To me, you can't have a conversation about work-life balance without using the word *family*. The point of making time for myself isn't so I can sit under a blanket and do the crossword puzzle, or catch up on my favorite TV shows. I've learned to leave work at work, and to stop myself from thinking constantly about my business, because it frees me up to spend more time—and better quality time—with my children, my husband, and my extended family, as well as making time to see friends and community members and form those connections that make my life rich and meaningful.

It was my family members who let me know that I was letting work creep into my life too often. I hadn't noticed—or maybe it's more accurate to say that it didn't really bother me.

The fact is, if you're passionate about your work, if you are deeply invested in doing the best you can, chances are you actually enjoy those long hours, those e-mails at midnight, and all the rest of it. And if you enjoy it, you probably won't mind all those little work tasks that creep into your home life.

My children talked to me about this. They'd ask me to put the computer down, saying, "Why do you have to send an e-mail at midnight?" If I got a call in the middle of the night from someone needing me to deal with an issue relating to a job, they might ask me in the morning, "Did you really need to pick up the phone at 2:30 in the morning?"

What made it so hard to detach from work was that there was always a good reason to be sending that e-mail that late at night. That ringing phone always seemed so urgent, and I always felt like I wanted to know about an issue right away instead of hearing about it in the morning.

Work was able to creep into my life because these little intrusions always felt too important to ignore.

But hearing these things from my family made me realize that spending time with them is important too. And just as important as making time to be with them is making sure those hours and days are *quality time*.

We're not talking about sitting on the couch and looking at spreadsheets on a laptop, checking e-mail on my phone. That's cheating, and when I would do those sorts of things I was cheating both them and myself. Even when I'd sit right next to them on the couch, watching television, I'd be thinking about how I was going to tackle my next big project. That was me taking time away from my family, being absent mentally. I wasn't focused on them, but on work.

Hearing from my family that I was working too much, that I was letting work interfere with our life together, had a powerful effect on me. As I said, if it was just a matter of me having time to knit a sweater or go to the movies, I might never have changed.

But hearing from my son that he felt like I wasn't listening, or seeing the look in my husband's face when I got up from the dinner table to take a work call, that really put things in perspective. It made me wonder, *Why am I running my own business if I'm not going to be free to enjoy the other parts of my life?*

And in a funny way, it felt like I was back to square one. Why did I want to run my own business in the first place? It certainly wasn't so I could worry about the company 24/7. I started my own business in part so I wouldn't be under anyone's control, so that no one would be able to take away my family's livelihood.

But even though I founded the company to avoid that negative, what made the business a success has been all the *positives* I've discovered along the way. I love the freedom of entrepreneurship, the ability to work from home, to go to breakfast with my children if I want to, to take a day or two for myself without having to answer to anyone.

But all that is meaningless if you don't *use* that freedom. If you always feel so suffocated by the need to work that you never take any time off—if you never even stop working—do you really have that freedom after all?

What Changed

The clearest sign that work had really overtaken the rest of my life was the fact that even when I was all caught up, when there were no pressing issues with an upcoming job, and my team was booked for weeks and months in advance, I still found ways to take attention away from my family and myself and focus it on work.

I might do a little internet research after dinner, looking for possible prospects to reach out to. Hours later, I'd still be at it, while my husband and children watched a movie in the other room. Or I'd come up with an idea for another business venture, an additional service that TBS might offer, and get caught up in looking into that possibility, finding people I might talk to about it. Suddenly it would be past midnight and everyone else was in bed.

There's really no better example than that of the double-edged sword of running your own business. On the one hand, it's a strong trait to always be on the lookout for ways to improve and grow, opportunities to open up new markets and create new avenues of income. But on the other hand, if you're going to be successful over the long haul, sometimes you've got to disconnect, decompress, and turn off that part of your brain.

So what changed? In a word, I gained the proper perspective on things. That had a lot to do with my family members letting me know that they wanted me to not only be there with them, they wanted me to take better care of myself.

But ultimately, what truly forced me to change was a health scare.

One day, during my annual exam prior to meeting with the doctor, the doctor discovered that my blood pressure was dangerously high. I was rushed to the hospital and diagnosed as having had a stroke three days earlier.

This incident forced me to reconsider my priorities, striving for more balance between my professional and personal lives. It also made me think about the future of the company and whether I want to do this forever.

I'm not the first person to see the light after something alarming happens with their health, but I can understand much better now how an experience like mine can change your life in a matter of seconds.

Because I've been working hard for such a long time, when I found myself forced to stop and deal with my health issue, my mind kept going. I caught myself thinking about work on the way to the doctor, or sitting in an office waiting for the doctor to see me. My dreams at night were about project planning, staffing, and paying my mortgage for the new year.

Somehow, catching myself thinking about work in these vital moments—or even while I was sleeping—when my focus should be 100 percent on my health and getting better, got through to me in a way my family members hadn't been able to. *What am I doing?* I asked myself.

By the time I was home, recuperating, I'd made up my mind. Right now I needed rest. What my body was demanding was that I go easy on it. It needed a break after all those years of going one hundred miles an hour from morning until late at night.

And I'd have to take it easy going forward. Free time is free time, and what I saw all too clearly was that I need it just as much as anybody else. There's a reason every society has a day when no one works, a day of rest. I truly believe I contributed to my illness through my hectic work schedule, by literally stressing myself out. Years of waking up at 6 a.m. and going all day, finally sleeping around 1 a.m., was bound to have an effect. I'm just thankful that when it caught up to me I was given another chance.

Striking the Right Balance

Not every entrepreneur is as lucky as I was. I've said it a number of times throughout the course of this book, but I am truly blessed that both my children are as interested and involved in the business as they are. Working beside them and training them to the point that they can keep things running smoothly if I want to take a meeting with a new client, work on my book, or just have some time to myself is such a gift to me.

It has never been more of a godsend than after my health scare. After I decided to work on getting my work-life balance in order, I didn't have to worry about what was going on with the business on a daily basis. I didn't feel the need to call and check in twenty times a day. I knew that I could entrust the business to my son and daughter completely, taking care of whatever I needed to without even thinking about the business. I know that if there's anything truly important, some pressing issue that needs my immediate decision, they'll get in touch with me; otherwise, they'll run things as they deem best. What a blessing!

At home, I've tried to create stricter rules for myself.

The Rewards of Finding the Right Balance

Taking time off for myself has taken some getting used to. As I said, I've been running TBS for more than twelve years now, keeping a frantic schedule and doing everything myself for most of that time. Sometimes habits are hard to break.

But knowing that the state of my health in the future could depend on breaking those habits is a powerful incentive. So is reflecting on what's truly important.

It's about family. But it's also about focusing on what I truly want to achieve and what I have to do to get there. All those years I was working sixteen-hour days, trying to build something for myself and my family, that's what I had to do to establish myself, to build a reputation that's known and trusted in my industry.

At this stage of my career, I can see further. I already told you I'm in the business of saving souls. What's become clearer to me recently is that I've got to protect myself so that I can continue saving souls for years to come. I can't do that if I'm physically incapacitated, or so burned out I can't muster the energy to do the work I want to do.

A wonderful benefit of changing my perspective on this balance between work and life is realizing all the ways that I can help myself, build stronger connections with the people I care about, and just generally improve my life simply by relaxing. Throughout my whole life, hard work has been valued, whether it was when I was working my first job as a cashier, interviewing for my first "real" office job, or when I started my own business. Working those long hours as an entrepreneur was a badge of honor.

The idea of kicking back beside a pool, taking a walk in the park, or enjoying any other kind of relaxing activity when I could be working always felt like an incredible indulgence, one that I couldn't afford. Now I get to savor those same kinds of activities, and it's actually *good* for me? That's something I could really get used to.

As I said earlier, taking time for myself and my family isn't just about forcing myself to be there for movie night or a cookout. It's about focusing on the *quality* of that time, too. I feel I've seen improvement in that area as well, now that I'm not so preoccupied with whatever happens to be going on at work in any given day. It takes practice, but once I started purposefully detaching from e-mail, and thinking less about this or that project, I found it easier to connect more deeply with my family and friends.

My friends and family agree. I've been told that in the past I've had a habit of taking a "business mind-set" into family situations, leading me to come off as controlling—as if I'm the boss at home as well as in the office. Just like working such long hours and letting work invade my home life, I can understand how that could happen. When you're the boss most of your waking hours, it's hard to turn off that switch.

But that doesn't mean that I can't change it. One of the real pleasures of taking time for myself is creating space to think about who I want to be at home and how I want to act. And so far I'm finding it's a welcome change to take that boss hat off and just be Tasha.

The only negative I can imagine, thinking about work-life balance, is the regret that I didn't do more years ago to create a healthy balance to my life. What might have turned out differently if I were better rested, more relaxed, etc., etc.?

But as you know by now, I don't let negatives or what-if questions nag at me. I don't really "do" regrets. All I can do with the time I have is enjoy it, sharing it with others and using it to build something that will empower others, inspire them, and save their souls.

So that's what I'm going to do.

Conclusion

Looking back over my life has been a transformative experience for me. Revisiting my past has allowed me to see the themes and qualities that have formed a connection over the years.

There's an incredible symmetry to the course my life has taken. After spending so much time alone in hospital rooms as a child, wishing for company, today I can enjoy the solitude and peace of being alone, and I can draw strength from it in other areas of my life.

In other cases, my life and myself are as far from that little girl as they can be. Years of internalizing the message that I was ugly and unwanted led me to develop the strength to push back against those messages, and to disregard people who repeated them to me. When you stop worrying about pleasing everyone, you can begin to please yourself—and, ironically, that's when people begin to be attracted to you. Today I'm confident in who I am and how I look, and I'm secure in my relationships to the people around me.

But there are deeper themes that have run throughout my entire life, connecting the trials and challenges and also the triumphs and joys.

Independence. Overcoming obstacles without making excuses. Helping others to help themselves.

These are the qualities that have stayed with me from my childhood to the present day, and have been part of the character and backbone that have allowed me to change from that lonely, overlooked little girl lying on her belly in the hospital room to the powerful, confident woman I am today.

Independence

While I was working on this book, the federal government was partially shut down for more than a month as Congress and the president negotiated over funding for border security.

It was almost enough to make me laugh. Here I was, describing how a desire for financial independence led me to strike out on my own, while the longest government shutdown in American history was unfolding.

But of course it was no laughing matter. Living near Washington, I saw too many friends and family members affected by the shutdown, and it even had an impact on TBS, which works closely with a number of federal agencies.

Given my story, though, I couldn't help but imagine *What if?* What if I'd never left my government job to found TBS? What if I was still there when the shutdown took place? Would I be just like one of the workers I saw on the news or heard interviewed on the radio, describing the financial hardships of missing multiple paychecks?

It made me anxious just thinking about it. Because I've been running my business for more than a dozen years now, my family and I have the financial security to weather a storm like the shutdown. Unlike so many of the families affected, we wouldn't have to worry about a mortgage payment or keeping the electricity on.

But far more valuable than financial security is the independence I felt, looking on as this story played out. I thought, This is exactly why I started TBS. So I'd never have to feel that a political argument playing out in the Capitol was going to make me question where the next meal was coming from, or whether I'd have to find a relative my children and I could stay with.

Writing this book has allowed me to see more clearly where that desire for independence came from, and in particular how I developed the strength to stand alone, to truly make the most of my independence. After all, it takes courage to go off on your own.

I see that when I look back over the chapters detailing the start of my business. I can still hear the things people said, the questions they asked me and the things they said behind my back. Was I crazy? I'd be living on someone's couch in a matter of weeks. I'd always regret leaving such a comfortable government job. Voices like that are exactly what an independent person learns to ignore, what he or she gains the strength to stand against.

That same strength has only grown as I've expanded my business and gained in knowledge and confidence over the last twelve years.

Here's another good example of how maintaining my independence has been absolutely critical in my life. During the final chapters of this book, I got some good news that I had honestly begun to wonder if I'd ever hear: I won three claims against the federal government and received payment for work TBS completed.

I'm not able to provide many details, but essentially TBS completed a substantial job for a client. We did our usual thorough, conscientious job, went home, and sent the client an invoice for payment.

And then nothing happened. No payment arrived.

As a business owner, this happens all the time. What was unusual in this case was the extreme amount of mistreatment that I and TBS received in our multiple attempts to be paid.

The other notable thing was that many people told me to forget about ever receiving payment. It just seemed to be known, even accepted, that when a federal government agency decides not to pay for services, the contractor faces poor odds of ever receiving that payment.

This was another instance when, listening to what people said and reading the general state of things, another person might have decided to cut their losses and focus on gaining new business, new jobs, new opportunities. No sense chasing after that payment when with every day our claim grew more and more distant, easier for the agency to forget about.

But that's what other people might have done. It's not what I do.

After contacting the Department of Justice and reaching out to my senator, Benjamin Louis Cardin, help me with my claims against the federal government.

The process was drawn out and emotionally taxing. Again, many people would have decided that the emotional investment, not to mention the expense of keeping a lawyer on the case, was not worth it, and let the matter go. I can't tell you how many times people gave me an odd look when I told them that TBS was suing the federal government. The general sense I got was that nobody did that, because the odds of winning were so low. And this all happened during the partial shutdown of the federal government!

But guess what? Within the last few weeks, I received notice that the government would be depositing a significant amount of funds into TBS's bank account: the original fee for services rendered, plus additional funds for interest.

Boom! When people talk about independence—mine, yours, or anyone else's—as blind stubbornness, or the refusal to listen to reason, a case like that one is what I think of.

You can say I'm stubborn. I know what's right and I know what I'm worth, and that's always worth standing up for, even if you stand alone.

Overcoming Obstacles without Making Excuses

At every step of my journey, I've documented the obstacles I've faced. Health problems at a young age kept me indoors and alienated me from my peers, even from my family members. A lack of love and support from family, the absence of my father in my life, had me questioning what I'd done to deserve the absence of love in my life. Being looked down on, doubted, and held to a higher standard than my business competitors threw additional obstacles in my path as I set out to build my business.

But what I learned when I was still a child is that obstacles can be opportunities. They're chances to grow stronger and to find out who you really are. Feeling the pain of surgeries and long recovery periods cured me of being afraid of physical pain. Being alone all the time gave me the strength to do what I wanted to do, even if I had to do it alone. And in time, I felt more confident in taking a stand because it no longer mattered to me whether I had a crowd behind me or not.

Those are all just stepping-stones to the biggest lesson of adversity, which is to face each new challenge with the certainty that you're going to overcome it. When you've overcome as much as I have, you no longer look at a stone in your path as something to trip over; it's just one more rock to kick out of the way as you walk steadily toward your goals.

Just as important as persevering is refusing to make excuses. If I can achieve something in my professional life, I let myself feel good about what I have accomplished. If I fail, or if I must pass up an opportunity because I don't think I can provide value to a customer, I take responsibility for that as well.

Lying to myself that my successes are all my own, but my shortcomings are the fault of someone else, doesn't build me up. It doesn't teach me anything, nor does it prepare me for the next challenge. It blinds me to the things that I need to improve in myself, my business, my approach to new opportunities. Passing the buck may feel good for a minute, but in the long term it is depriving me of the chance to grow even stronger.

The claims against the federal government that I mentioned above are just one recent example of how I have faced down an obstacle without making excuses. In many ways, it would have been easier to simply forget about that money, complaining and growing bitter about the wrong that had been done.

I chose not to do that. It is the choices we make that determine who we are, and I choose to be the kind of person who refuses to allow a client to eschew their obligation to pay me and my staff for work done, and done well.

Then there's the small stroke that I mentioned in the previous chapter, describing how it caused me to reconsider my priorities and the balance between my professional and personal lives.

One thing it *didn't* do, though, was discourage me. There was bound to be a solution to this problem—I was working too much and it was affecting my health and the quality of my life—and I knew I would find it.

And as far as making excuses, it was clear that no one but me was responsible for working so hard for so long.

In this case, in fact, I was blessed to be surrounded by family members who had been telling me for years to take it slow. Being forced to stop and see what I was doing to myself by keeping the relentless schedule that I keep helped open my eyes to how much the people in my life cared about me.

And I was truly blessed that my children know the company so well and were available to step up and run day-to-day operations while I rested.

When you refuse to make excuses, I've found, you also become more aware of all that you have to be grateful for.

Helping Others to Help Themselves

The final theme that's connected the different parts of my life may just be the most important to me.

As I look back at my life, I see my independence and my ability to overcome obstacles as paving the way for me to help others. In other words, my whole life I've been developing the strength and experience I've needed to build my own platform, one which I can use to help me pull others up out of their own difficult circumstances.

It's not enough to have the strength to stand alone, or to overcome whatever life throws at you, if it doesn't serve a higher purpose.

The key story of my life up to this moment is of getting up on my own two feet and then building the strength to lift others up. It's not about glorifying myself, or handing out favors, but about glorifying God and allowing the people I help to provide for themselves and their families.

And of course the process doesn't end there: when I lift others up, my greatest desire is that they in turn will gain the strength to reach back and lift up the people around them. That's how true, lasting change takes place, and while all it takes is one person to get it started, that change requires many people to keep it going, to build on that first little bit of momentum, and in so doing to make a real, lasting difference.

That desire to help others has manifested itself over time in the way I run my business, through hiring recently returned citizens. It's come out in the nonprofit organization I founded for the express purpose of giving those returning citizens the opportunities they need to reintegrate into society. It's come out in the mentoring relationships I've formed with young people just starting out on the path of entrepreneurship.

Making connections and sowing the seeds of entrepreneurship and the empowerment it can offer is so much more than I ever imagined for myself. Even when I first began my business, I never pictured myself standing up on a stage and offering inspiration to others. And as a little girl lying on her belly in a hospital room, I couldn't have imagined having the confidence to walk across a stage, look out at an audience of a hundred or more people, and tell them about my life.

But that's just what I'm doing, and these first speeches and presentations are just the start.

As a result of my speaking engagements, as well as through my presence in the community, a number of people have reached out for help starting their own businesses. Many of these people don't know where to begin, or find themselves desperately confused by the red tape and impenetrable jargon they encounter when they enter the business world (especially those with an interest in working with the federal government).

I'm happy to help. A number of these would-be entrepreneurs offer to pay me a fee, but I always turn them down. Mentoring, giving my counsel, these are activities that do me good, and I know that to try to profit from these things would make them far less satisfying.

As I said earlier, what is the purpose of attaining the knowledge and experience I have, or building the platform from which to reach an expanded audience, if my purpose isn't to help others?

Revisiting the Past

Writing this book has required me to look back, to walk down Memory Lane and revisit all the avenues of my past. It hasn't always been comfortable to revisit some of these memories, especially from my childhood.

But one thing I've learned from the experience is that even if you've made mistakes in your life, it is a tremendous blessing to be able to look back and feel that you can be proud of who you are and what you've done. To see the path my life has taken me on, from a childhood spent hidden away in hospital rooms to an adulthood in which I have become stronger than I ever thought possible, is such an incredible blessing.

Just as transformative and as important, though, is the chance that all this reflection has given me to re-evaluate the events of my life and the people in it and, in many cases, to consider new ways to approach those people. At times I've found it hard to forgive and forget, but in writing this book I came to understand the viewpoint of some of those people, and I've challenged myself to reach out to some of them to reopen the lines of communication.

Reflecting on my own experiences as a mother, for example, has allowed me to see my mother's behavior in a new light. What happened, happened. As I described in an earlier chapter, I've chosen to use the experience of my childhood to identify the love I wish I'd had and to make sure to pass that on to my own children. But as I set down those thoughts, I found it growing easier to understand why my mother acted the way she did, and even to bring some of this up in conversation. I'm not going to say that everything is perfect now, but the relief at simply talking about these things, clearing the air after so much time, is colossal.

As I wrote in the last section, we choose what kind of people to be by what we do, and in going over the past I have recognized that I have the opportunity to be a bigger person by opening those avenues of communication rather than stewing over what happened and what might have been.

Looking toward the Future

The other effect of going over my past and reviewing the course of my life is to make me even more excited for the future—the future of my business. The future of my work in the community. But most of all, the future of my family. When I turn away from the past and try to look into the future, I see nothing but opportunity ahead.

If there's one thing I'd want to repeat at the conclusion of this book, it's how grateful I am to have the children I have, how happy they've made me through the years. To work beside them, to be able not only to speak to them like the intelligent and hardworking people that they are, but to leave things in their command knowing that my business is in good hands—it's a blessing for which I thank God every day of my life.

And this blessing gives me the kind of freedom to explore new opportunities and partnerships on a scale I never would have imagined when I was bidding for those first jobs, just starting out in business.

As I write this, TBS has already confirmed nearly $300,000 in contracts for the upcoming year, despite the fact that we're barely six weeks into the new year.

Looking back on the first twelve years of TBS's existence, I'm astonished at how far we've come and how much we've accomplished. Looking ahead, I can hardly imagine how much more we are poised to achieve.

Of course, I'd have to be naïve to look into the future and imagine that it will be nothing but positives, a smooth road paved only with opportunities, free of challenges or obstacles. By this point in my career, I know to expect hardships, to expect snags and unforeseen problems.

But I also know what I've been through, and I know what I'm capable of.

I'm stronger for everything I have experienced, but I'm stronger still because of the purpose I've discovered and refined along the way. While providing for my children was a powerful motivator when I was just starting out, today I'm out there trying to save souls, and there's no more powerful motivation than that.

With a *why* like that, there's nothing I can't do.

About the Author

Tasha Berry grew up in the Washington, D.C., area, raised by a single mother. Her first memories are of painful hospital visits to treat her gigantic congenital nevomelanocytic nevus, a skin condition that left her back covered with moles and required doctors to scrape off the skin, replacing it with skin taken from the backs of her legs.

From this early adversity and pain, Tasha drew the internal strength to endure pain, isolation, and emotional neglect. Blessed with a strong work ethic, she brought money into the family beginning at age fourteen, often caring for her younger siblings.

After a semester at college, Tasha returned home inspired with newfound confidence and soon began a successful career working in the federal government, one that lasted ten years. But after having two children, her priorities shifted and she found herself increasingly bothered by the knowledge that her boss, or an act of Congress, could deny her the ability to support her family.

She quit her job and set out on her own, founding a company, TBS Facility Services Group, that organizes and carries out moving duties for government agencies. After a series of terrific, high-profile successes, including moving jobs for the Department of Transportation and the Gaylord National Hotel, TBS grew rapidly, buoyed by its stellar reputation. Today, the company routinely earns over $1 million annually in revenue.

Having achieved her goal of financial independence, Tasha sought out ways to make her success meaningful and sustained. She taught her children the art of entrepreneurship and entrusted major parts of TBS's business to them, supported neighbors and family by hiring them as movers, and founded a nonprofit organization, the Phoenix Reintegration Project, that offers free job training to those recently returned from incarceration.

At every step, the "negatives" that once defined Tasha have guided her. From her sense of loneliness, she draws the strength to stand alone. From feeling isolated, she sees the value in community. And from recognizing the love she never received, she can better offer that same love to her children.

She's found meaning in reaching back to help those around her. Or as she likes to say, she's in the business of saving souls.